IF YOU
COULD HAVE
ANYTHING...

IF YOU COULD HAVE

ANYTHING...

...What Would It Be?

Jo De Rosa

First Published in Canada 2012 by Influence Publishing

Graphic Design and Layout: Greg Salisbury

Testimonials

Meg Meagher (Actress)

"I first met Jo about five years ago when I responded to an advert at my local gym for a one to one yoga session. Little did I know that this meeting, (which I assumed was another way to get fit!) would have such a major impact on every area of my life. Not only did my body become more toned and fit, but I was introduced to the practice of meditation and mindfulness which go hand in hand with Jo's yoga practice. Very rapidly, my body and my outlook on life began to change. I was more aware of how I treated my body and also something which I had never been aware of before, I started to listen to that small voice within which guided me to make the right decisions in all areas of my life. I learnt about detoxing my body - kindly imparted to me from Jo's time in Thailand - and her amazing yoga retreats that I attended to refresh and reconnect. Seeing other people change for the better over a weekend retreat was a joy.

Watching Jo's journey unfold, from starting her own business, meeting the love of her life and become a successful author has been nothing but inspiring as she continues to grow in every area of her life. I know that anyone reading about Jo's amazing journey will be inspired to know that anything is possible and life can be truly great if we allow it.

This I have learnt from Jo who has been an amazing teacher, mentor and friend."

Danny Meehan (Service Manager)

"My experiences with Jo whether it be the yoga classes I attend, the fun and creative yoga class my seven and nine year old daughters attended, or just our one to one conversations have always been insightful and rewarding. Jo always seems to have a deep understanding of life's trials and tribulations, and gifts those around her with the positivity and energy she seems to posses herself in abundance."

Sue Rice (HR Manager)

"I met Jo 2 ½ years ago when I moved to Ware and embarked on her Thursday yoga class at Wodson Park. After spending 15 years attending a yoga class in London, I was slightly apprehensive about starting with a new teacher. But I needn't have worried as I was soon put at ease with Jo's relaxed teaching style.

After hearing so much about Jo's yoga retreats, I decided to experience one for myself. So in February 2012, I arrived at a beautiful house in Norfolk for the weekend, not really knowing what to expect.

I spent the next 48 hours immersed in yoga, meditation, relaxation, and good company. The retreat for me was life altering and absolutely amazing. Jo teaches in a very calm and supportive way that makes you feel better about life, and shows you how you can use the practice to overcome obstacles in your life. I left the retreat feeling like a new woman. This feeling stayed with me for 3 months after, and is still there in the background of my life today.

As a booster I also attended one of Jo's full day workshops. The workshop came at a time when I was going through some major upheavals in my life. After my practice with Jo I left feeling refreshed, positive and ready to face the world again.

I realised after the retreat that I always want some form of yoga practice in my life, as it can help me get off the 'hamster wheel' and get some 'me' time -and that its ok to do that. As a busy working mum of twins, I continue to practice and use yoga and meditation to deal with the stresses and strains in my daily world.

Jo is a truly inspiring person, who radiates positive energy, and is someone I want to be around. Whenever I start feeling overwhelmed by life, I up my yoga and meditation practice and life feels calmer again. Jo has given me the tools to do that, and for that I am truly grateful.

Thank you Jo for helping me enter your world (for some of the time anyway!)."

Emily Mayers (Risk Assessor)

"Jo De Rosa is an inspiring yoga teacher, trusted adviser and great friend.

Her compassion and strength of character has given me courage through difficult times. Her unique style of teaching and coaching has transformed my yoga practice and helped me achieve an internal calm. My daughter loves her classes and it's great to know that she is gaining the positive effects of yoga at such a young age in such a busy world."

Sam Marriot (Counsellor)

"I started going to Jo De Rosa for semi-private yoga sessions because I had found myself lost and disconnected, mind, body and soul. Through these sessions and Jo's wisdom, insights and patience, I have found myself coming back together. I suspect in our current culture the head being separate from the body causes fear, anger and greed and that any activity that seeks to reintegrate our body and mind should be taken seriously.

I have learnt about my human responsibility to listen to myself, and the impact I make. I also take my children to see Jo so that through yoga and meditation, they may grow and maintain their own sense of self.

My hope is that Jo's book won't be just a book, but a recipe for humanity to move forward, one individual at a time."

Vicki Riddell (Insurance Broker)

"I always feel relaxed, stronger, and at peace after one of Jo's yoga sessions. She has a lovely way of making the mind and body work in

harmony without you even knowing it. I know I can face whatever life throws at me, however difficult, because I have learned the skills needed to put my yoga practice into everyday life."

Nadine Davies (Antique Dealer)

"Jo is a truly gifted teacher whose approach is wonderfully calming and nurturing. Her meditation techniques restore and revive deflated bodies, and over worked minds are left filled with positive and inspirational thoughts. I very much look forward to reading her first novel and seeing how these special qualities manifest themselves in print. Good Luck!"

John Halliday (Railway Safety Controller)

"Having had the benefit of being one of Jo's private students, I believe I am in a good position (no pun intended) to remark how thorough Jo is in her explanations and guidance during yoga and meditation practice.

Also I have been fortunate enough to have experienced a full day on one of Jo's informative, instructive and enjoyable workshops. It gave me a big leap forward in my practice and knowledge, and is wholly recommended as a start into yoga practice if one is not sure how to find out more in a relaxed and friendly atmosphere. I felt it good enough for my 11 year old daughter and her mother to attend as a gift, and both thoroughly enjoyed their day."

Dedication

To anyone that has ever thought:
"There must be more than this"
Because there is!

Life is as amazing as you dare to imagine it, why don't you
ask yourself this question right now:
"If I Could Have Anything... What Would It Be?"

Acknowledgements

To Dominic my fabulous husband, who loves me unconditionally for who I am, and gives me the space I need to be me. Without him this book would have been very different, and I thank him for his input, love and acceptance.

To my wonderful sister George, who will always be my soul-sister. I apologise to you for some of my appalling behaviour in the past, and thank you for always supporting, guiding, and loving me so beautifully. To J too for being such a rock.

To my parents Jan and Keith who also had to put up with some pretty horrific tantrums all the way up until I was 17 and was 'given my freedom!' They stand strong behind me always, forever believing in my new projects and businesses and allowing me to be free. I love them and thank them wholeheartedly.

To my stepchildren who have taught me lessons I never thought I would learn, and stretched me beyond belief. They are such good kids and I hope I can guide and support them always.

I thank Phil for my first ever yoga class where I literally 'knew' in that instance that my life was about to change and go off in a new direction. Suzie was first to train me in the beautiful surroundings of Spa Samui, Thailand, and her gentle and thorough approach set standards high in my new teaching role. Sharat inspired me further in India with his unusual angle on what I was already teaching, and I will always feel indebted to his deep knowledge and love of yoga, which has passed to so many students of mine also.

Gemma must have a special mention for without her I would never have taken up my first yoga class! She bugged me to join her and in the end I complied –I thank her from the bottom of my heart.

I am lucky to have many friends who inspire me and nurture my continued growth. Vena, Maia, Mandy, Mel, Megan, Al, and Louise, all of whom have grown with me through the years.

I would like to thank Ginny who did a beautiful job of editing my first book, and Julie who guided me so expertly through the writing process.

I'd like to also thank Rachel, who inspires and pushes me to keep thinking outside the box and get out of my comfort zone.

Of course I'd like to thank my extended family and friends who are always there for me.

Lastly thank you to my students who make it all so worthwhile. After a long day of teaching, I go to bed happy in the knowledge that I have successfully passed on the information I have gathered, and which has enriched my own life, onward and outward.

Contents

Foreword

"If you could have anything what would it be?" It's a question that very few people dare to dream about, trapped in a world of limiting beliefs about what is possible/practical/achievable for them, stuck in jobs they hate and in relationships that no longer serve them. Drowning out the little voice that says 'There must be more to life than this?' with booze and drugs and mindless soap operas on TV.

Each of the characters in this book starts out unhappy and unfulfilled with their life. And each has the courage to reach out to find the answers. But it all starts with the belief that somewhere out there is something far better for them.

Jo De Rosa is living testimony to the ability to turn everything around.

She has completely transformed her own former life of self-abuse, replacing her unhealthy addiction to drink, drugs and cigarettes with a healthy addiction to yoga, meditation and clean living.

The abusive and controlling former boyfriend has been replaced by a wonderful, good-looking and supportive husband.

And from a place of struggle around money she's now in flow.

What's more, Jo has a body to die for and is as powerful on the inside (mentally) as she is on the outside (physically).

Jo's book will demonstrate to you that anything is possible. And it will give you the inspiration (as well as a kick in the butt) to finally let go of everything that isn't working in your life.

It's fear that keeps us in prisons of our own making, yet when we start to open up to the adventure of life - and live from a place of faith in the power of the Universe - that's when the magic really begins.

So, if you could have anything what would it be?

Rachel Elnaugh: Entrepreneur, Dragons' Den Star and Transformational Coach. www.rachelelnaugh.com

Chapter One

Rob

Coked Up On Christmas Day

"You are what you do, not what you say you'll do."
Carl Jung

Rob hated having an addictive personality. He always seemed to be addicted to something and once he battled one demon, another would quickly jump into its shoes.

Smoking had been the most difficult demon he had successfully overcome to date, but it had taken the best part of 10 years of to-ing and fro-ing before he could finally call himself a non-smoker. And it had driven him almost mad during the process simply because it made no sense. He hated every cigarette he smoked so why keep doing it??!!

However, slowly over the years he tackled each one, and found more and more contentment and happiness as he did.

Life is one long party

Rob's addiction career spanned more than 20 years and the first addiction he successfully conquered was cocaine.

Rob and Nikky had a very unhealthy relationship which centred around their love of partying and drug taking at the weekend. They playfully called themselves weekend junkies, which over their years together became the only time they liked and could actually talk to each other.

They had met at Gas on the London club scene, and being on the same circuit they had lots of mutual friends. Rob had dark skin and hair and had been instantly attracted to blond, skinny Nikky. When they got together they were both high on ecstasy, and when they finally split up they were also on this same drug. They would dance for hours in some of London's trendiest club nights.

Nikky was also a serious puff junkie. Rob didn't really like being stoned but kind of went along with it and spent a number of years completely out of it. Years later he realised that he'd only ever seen Nikky as herself (without *any* drugs) a couple of times, and she wasn't very nice at all.

They also both developed a very unhealthy taste for cocaine and gradually lessened their pill intake and upped the coke.

Coke is a very difficult drug to take when in a club, as it needs to be chopped (with a credit card) and placed into a neat line ready to be snorted via a rolled up note. Rob and Nikky would sometimes spend the majority of their time queuing for and using the toilet, and no sooner back on the dance floor, than the urge for another hit would arise.

Getting high

As their relationship deteriorated, and their coke habit spiralled out of control, they started to go out less and stay at home more so that they could do more coke. There were no restrictions at home and it was so much easier snorting line after line in their living room. The coke made them more talkative and interested in each other, and they would literally catch up on the whole week where they had been too stoned each night to talk about their day at work. Perhaps that was one of the reasons they continued on this dangerous trajectory, but for Rob it was mainly and simply because he loved getting high.

As it turned out Rob would spend most of his life looking for some sort of lift.

He worked hard all week and told himself he deserved a release and to feel really good. They would get their Saturday night drugs mid week, and sometimes just knowing the coke was in the flat would be too much for them to resist, and they would stay up all night and have to either go to work high or phone in sick. Then they would also have to buy more drugs for the weekend. Rob knew it was not a good situation but at that time was powerless to stop it.

Coked up on Christmas Day

The turning point for Rob came one Christmas when he and Nikky had bought a large amount of cocaine for the Christmas period and done most of it on Christmas Eve! By 11am on Christmas morning Rob knew he was so high there was no way he could face his family for Christmas dinner and festivities. They had not even gone out that night, just stayed in alone doing drugs. Rob phoned his Mum and blagged illness. His Mum wanted to come over later with turkey leftovers and Rob had to insist she didn't. He really didn't want her to see him like this. Nikky decided she'd go to her family's dinner and left Rob alone on Christmas day high as a kite having had no sleep the night before. It was an all time low and he made the decision then that he needed to sort his life out. He'd never spent Christmas day without his family and alone before. But for now he started to chop up another line....

Ending your relationship on ecstasy

It took a few months but he gradually came around to the idea that he and Nikky definitely did not bring out the best in each other, and their relationship had reached its use by date.

He broke the news to Nikky one night while they were at a friends party and taking ecstasy. They were very chatty pills and he'd said the words before he'd thought of the consequences. It was like that sometimes on pills, you could talk to complete strangers about the most personal and intimate details of yourself.

They lived together, had a cat together and had become more like brother and sister. They decided that night that she would move back in with her parents immediately while he took care of the flat, which they rented in his name.

It had all happened really quickly and he had to give his landlord a months notice, so Rob took this time to reflect on the best way to move away from the club and drug scene. As soon as Nikky moved out the puffing stopped as he'd never enjoyed it anyway, but coke was near enough impossible to resist when it was in front of him. He knew he needed to remove himself from it completely, but how?

To untangle himself from the unhealthy web he had spun, Rob took the drastic step of moving to a completely new area. He'd done this before a few years earlier and knew it was a great way of leaving behind baggage that you didn't want to haul around.

This time he was leaving behind Nikky and coke. The Nikky part was actually quite easy because their relationship had been dead for a long time, but ridding cocaine from his life meant not seeing *a lot* of his friends. Many of his friendships were closely woven with drugs and he was making a clean break as it was the only way.

If he wanted to see any of these people again it would have to be in a 'safe' environment where drugs were not being consumed. Later he would look back on some of these friendships and realise that they were only held together by drug glue, and once drugs were taken out of the equation he really didn't miss these people at all.

As the months wore on, he could now see the world in a much different way, like someone had given him a pair of rose tinted glasses and he couldn't believe how great this life looked.

In the past the whole weekend had been centred on drug taking with Sunday whizzing past in a spaced out state and trying to eat, Monday in a deep dark depression, Tuesday slightly better, Wednesday better still, Thursday and Friday quite good, then start the cycle all over again on Saturday. Rob would just start to feel himself again on Friday before the next onslaught!

Now, post drugs he had the whole weekend to enjoy, and experienced Sundays for the first time since he was a child.

Falling off the coke wagon

Of course he did fall off the coke wagon a few times over the coming months and years, but it was easier now to get back up, shake yourself down and vow to try harder next time, and because he no longer kept drug-type company, these rare occasions were purely one offs.

Rob was sometimes really hard on himself, however, and would wake up angry that he'd had a few lines. But a few lines was all he could manage these days. If he thought back to the height of his addiction and how much of that filth he could shovel up his nose in one night, it actually really frightened him. He was very lucky that he'd not caused serious injury to himself.

Three steps forward, three steps back.

Three steps forward, two steps back, yay!

He would remind himself he was doing really well, to not beat himself up so much and to chill-out.

It did get easier with time and once Rob had been out of the scene for a year he gained in confidence so much that he was ready for the next addiction to be tackled…..

If he could give up smoking then ANYONE could!

Throughout his smoking career the first thing Rob did in the morning was have a cigarette. Then he would smoke all through the day and night finishing off with the last cigarette of the day in bed. Some female companions had found his habit absolutely disgusting, while others happily joined in with his smoking in bed. He knew it was foul, but he just couldn't help himself.

When he first tried to give up he replaced tobacco for marijuana by making pure weed joints. However, he soon realised that he couldn't hold down his job or stay sane doing that, so the next step was cutting down. But cutting down just meant that he spent all day wishing and waiting for his next hit of nicotine, and so he made the decision that he had to stop completely.

Cold turkey was the only way

People talk about having an addictive personality, and he knew he had one as he couldn't do anything by halves. Cutting down was out of the question so he set himself a stopping date one week later. In the coming seven days he smoked more than he ever had before knowing that the fateful day was growing ever closer. It got so bad two days before that he was actually sick from smoking too many ciggies. He was disgusted, once again, with himself. Why on earth had he done that to himself? His quit day arrived and he felt very confident in the morning, but as the day wore on and his withdraw became unbearable, he reached for what gave him comfort. As soon as he'd smoked that first cigarette he felt remorse and then anger at himself for being so weak. Why had he just done exactly the opposite of what he really wanted for himself?

Finally getting somewhere

So the cycle continued and for the time being he carried on smoking then someone told him about a great book that had really helped them to quit. Rob literally ran to the book shop to purchase Alan Carr's *Easy Way to Stop Smoking*. In it the reader is advised to continue to smoke until the book is finished, and your last cigarette is smoked whilst reading the last chapter. Rob had his new quit day!

The book made so much sense and gave loads of really interesting facts and home truths about smoking. As he neared the end of the book Rob found himself getting quite excited about stopping. Day one, two and three were fine, but day four was a massive struggle and Rob just couldn't get through it without a cigarette. He plunged into a deep depression and felt resentful, upset and angry with his failure.

This pattern of stopping for a couple of days and starting again went on for the next six months, then a breakthrough! Rob made it through the first week, then the first month, and easily reached the 11-month mark without a single drag on a cigarette. He felt truly proud of his achievement, and his body thanked him too. He had more energy and could think so clearly, he loved it. But unfortunately he got a bit cocky one night when he'd had a few too many beers and vodkas and ponced a cigarette off a friend. He reasoned that he was nearly at the one year mark, and this was just one cigarette. He took it home, lay down on his sofa, and slowly and fully smoked that cigarette. He pulled the filthy smoke deep into his lungs and watched the path the smoke made as he blew it out again. He could feel the drug hitting his system and travel to his brain where he began to feel dizzy. It was like every cell in his body was fizzing and enjoying the act of smoking. He went to bed satisfied, light headed and sure this was a one-off event.

The next morning the monster was back.

It was like he was having an outer body experience as he walked the next morning to the shop and bought a packet of Marlborough Lights. He watched himself make the journey, make the purchase, open the packet and smoke six in quick succession.

How stupid he was!

He was catapulted straight back to where he had been 11 months ago. All that fantastic work he'd achieved, down the toilet, where he was about to be sick from nicotine overload.

The disappointment was palpable. He was shocked that he could go so far into the non-smoking world and come tumbling back to addiction so easily and readily.

He hated himself and he hated cigarettes.

He gave up giving up for the next few months, he just couldn't bear to go through the withdrawal period again just yet, as it seemed that each withdrawal was harder than previous efforts. He knew you had to do it when you felt ready, and right now he had no strength.

Chewing your drug rather than smoking it

Chapter One

Nicotine Replacement Therapy became the latest method to assist in stopping smoking, and Rob got right on board. He purchased a pack of nicotine chewing gum and had the first one after his breakfast one day. It was disgusting and he spat it out. It tasted like eating an ashtray! The nicotine withdrawal really kicked in then and he tried another gum. He slowly chewed, and when the flavour started to release and become intense, he pushed the gum down between his lower right gum and face to let the nicotine soak down into his bloodstream, as the instruction booklet advised. He was amazed because his longing to smoke had gone completely. Wow, these things really work! Rob spent the next week chewing gum and not smoking, and was really happy. Gone were the cravings and the bad moods, he was *not smoking and happy*, four words he did not expect to be saying in one sentence.

OK, his jaw ached, but, hey, he didn't even want a cigarette.

This went on for around four months, until someone asked him for a chewing gum down the pub and Rob had to explain that he was chewing no ordinary gum. A conversation ensued about chewing nicotine and Rob was told there was a big chance of contracting mouth cancer from his new habit. His acquaintance told him that because the gum was placed and held against his gum so the nicotine can ooze out and into his body, this raised the chance of mouth cancer.

Rob was devastated and knew he had to come up with another plan to stop smoking. He purchased some ordinary gum and decided he would swap to this, by cutting down to just a few nicotine hits per day.

Easier said than done. And he had to admit that he had been chewing the nicotine gum even when he had no urge for a cigarette, simply to get a high from the gum. He was well and truly hooked. The ordinary gum tasted awful as he just wanted the nicotine.

Rob now had the unenviable task of giving up nicotine again, the only difference this time was it was gum rather than cigarettes. He was, in fact, no further forward than he had been years earlier when he first decided to stop smoking.

The problem he now had was he really didn't want to stop chewing the gum as it tasted so great, had none of the other harmful ingredients that cigarettes contain, and actually made him feel slightly high. Oh dear, maybe swapping one nicotine product for another really wasn't going to work after all. (It's so obvious in hindsight!)

Rob still couldn't see the sky for the clouds, and went and bought some nicotine patches. He reasoned that perhaps it was the habit of chewing the gum at certain times was what was holding him back from being free, and stupidly wore a patch, chewed the gum, and smoked the odd cigarette also over the next few months.

Rob knew by now that Nicotine Replacement Therapy did NOT work for him. The last three weeks had been off ciggies, just chewing gum and the first day without gum and he was smoking again. The only way was cold turkey, he knew this already, but he felt like he'd just officially proved it!

It had now been a ridiculous 10 years of trying to quit and Rob had tried pills to take away the craving, hypnotherapy, acupuncture, and even joined an online support group, and was still unsuccessful. He had tried everything. He felt so run down by the whole thing. He felt pathetic for doing the very thing that he wanted to not do. He thought about smoking all the time, it was driving him crazy. It was so frustrating. Like trying to break out of a cage. The only thing was he had the key, knew what he needed to do, but just couldn't bring himself to put the key in the lock, turn it, and allow freedom.

And he had tasted it before, many times, for varying lengths of time and freedom felt amazing. In contrast, addiction made him feel powerless and weak.

Rob set himself a new quit date. He guessed over the past 10 years this was probably the one millionth quit date, but now he was really sick of it and the 10th anniversary had really hit home how ridiculous it all was. Did he want to quit? YES!

So just bloody do it then

He was ready to rid his body of the poison, and the only way he could do that was first to give up the gum and switch back to the ciggies. The gum was delicious and gave him no incentive to stop, the cigarettes on the other hand were filthy and he absolutely hated smoking them.

He knew he would be smoking more as the quit day approached and he was not wrong. He even started buying a stronger brand to make the smoking experience even more unpleasant, and spent quite a few evenings puking because he'd smoked too much. Quit day was 13th June 2006 and he couldn't wait. He was ready.

Thank you Maia

Rob decided to have a small tattoo on the inside of his right wrist located at the acupressure point of the liver. He'd had quite a few sessions of acupuncture with Maia over the last couple of years and she had shown him where this spot was. She had said that when he felt an addictive urge to smoke, drink, or do drugs of any kind, he could lightly press on this point to 'cool' the liver and reduce the craving. He was planning on using this method over the next few days. The tattoo was a small heart, as he now wanted to start taking care of himself instead of filling up his body with poisons and toxins which he had been consuming ever since he was 14 or 15. He had a longing to be healthy and happy and prove to himself and others that he could do this.

He'd chosen that particular date because he knew he was going to be very busy. He was starting a new job, which would require evening research at home. He could plunge himself into this new work and direct his energy into something useful. He was not planning on lazing around feeling sorry for himself and his addiction any more, this was a new start.

The planning paid off, and even though it was not always easy, Rob coped really well and didn't smoke for the first month. He avoided certain places during this time, places where he knew he would struggle. Then as his confidence grew, he realised that he could actually cope in any situation. In fact he seemed to get stronger and dare he say it, *it was easy!* He was scared of saying that, though, as he'd been smug and complacent before which had blown up in his face and sent him straight back to the corner shop.

Drinking was the biggest challenge as the association with smoking was very strong. He had his weakest moments when he was tanked up, but luckily English law had changed and you could no longer smoke in pubs, clubs and restaurants. This made life much easier for the fledgling non-smoker as he would have to brave the cold and rain to smoke outside.

Every time he made it past a craving, a night out, or a situation where he knew it would be difficult, he became stronger and knew he was getting closer to his ultimate goal. He started to believe that he could really do it, but he was not going to fall into the complacency trap again.

The months passed, his new job was going well and he was not smoking. Rob was anxious to get past 11 months as it was a huge marker for him. When he did finally pass the one-year finish line he felt like he'd won the gold medal. He stood on the podium in his mind and saw and heard everyone cheering, and the cheers were for overcoming all the doubts he'd had about himself over the past 10 years of trying to stop smoking. He had conquered his demons and proved to himself that he could achieve anything.

The gold medal of freedom

Rob no longer felt tortured as he was now free.

It was strange, once he had not smoked a single cigarette in one year, he no longer had *any cravings*. Even when he was drinking heavily they had gone! Now the smell of cigarette smoke bothered him and made him feel unwell. He couldn't believe how much of that filth he had systematically put into his body over the years. Now the smell of just one cigarette turned his stomach.

He was becoming one of those annoying ex-smokers. You know, the ones who pull a face and wave their hand in front of their face in disgust around smokers. He laughed to himself as he wouldn't have believed it possible one year ago.

As time progressed to five years of smoking abstention Rob never went backwards. If only he had known how it felt to be free of this drug back then when he was struggling so badly. If someone back then had given him the body he was in now, for him to feel what good health and mental freedom felt like, then he would have given up years before.

I'm never going to drink again!

The years passed by and he thought about smoking less and less. Rob married Annabel and life calmed down and, dare he say, became 'normal'. His drinking, however, increased. But this addiction was one which was very socially acceptable, and would prove to be the most difficult to get under control.

It had been a particularly heavy night of drinking until 4am that was the final straw for Rob. He didn't actually feel human, it was like something had taken over his mind and body and nothing was working properly. Why, oh why, had he done this to himself? It made no sense to him, and to top it off he had spent a shit load of money last night. He decided that he was going to lay off the sauce for one month and see how it went. He had made many similar, unsuccessful decisions not to drink before and even though he wanted to do this so badly he knew it was not going to be easy. He and the missus liked to share a bottle of wine in the evenings, so it wasn't just the big events but the everyday drinking too. He knew his wife wouldn't stop drinking with him, she didn't want or need to, it was him that had the problem.

Am I an alcoholic?

What makes someone an alcoholic? What are the rules of alcoholism? How much do you need to drink, and how regularly, to be classed an alcoholic?

Rob drank a bottle of wine with Sunday lunch and on a Wednesday night with the wife, three or four pints at the pub on a Friday with the boys and another bottle of wine on Saturday night at least. It wasn't huge amounts but it was consistently drinking four out of seven days a week, every week, with regular sessions of up to three bottles of wine, a few pints, then some shots at the weekend when out with friends. Rob thought that when alcohol became a problem in your life, and you found it difficult to give up, that was when you could call yourself an alcoholic, and he knew he had a problem with alcohol. Others may have thought otherwise, but that didn't matter to Rob, he wanted to change his drinking habits and attempts to 'cut down' were successful for a short period but always ended up back to where he started *or worse*. Anyway, it was just a label and didn't really matter. The simple fact was that Rob was addicted, and how much and how often was actually of little importance. He knew that when he had that poison in his system he lost control, and *that* was where his problem lay.

Even his wife thought he was being ridiculous when he discussed his addiction with her:

"You are not an alcoholic!" she would say.

"But I have a problem and drinking makes me feel unhappy and depressed," he'd reply,

"Don't drink as much then. You sometimes don't know when to stop, that's all."

"Exactly! I have no off switch. God forgot to give me the off switch!"

"And I have no idea why you're reading that AA blue book either."

"Because it helps me to make sense of what I'm feeling and how to cope."

In truth Annabel didn't drink much less than he did but she seemed to not have a problem with it or be bothered by it, and it just didn't seem to affect her at all. She slept as normal, woke up as normal, and got on with her day. He on the other hand was the complete opposite. He never got a decent night's sleep if he'd been drinking, felt like crap in the morning, and the depression lasted until the next drinking session. It was pretty much constant.

He had abstained in the past after other overindulgent episodes and the two things that struck him most was how deeply he slept and how clear his mind was with no alcohol in his system. Yes he was gagging for a drink at the end of the abstention period and as soon as it crossed his lips the clarity of mind was gone and he'd toss and turn all that night, and was back to where he started.

Since he had stopped smoking and taking cocaine five years

ago the drinking had escalated, and he found himself in a dance of binging and abstaining, back and forth between the two. The thing was he really didn't like himself when he'd had a drink as he got loud and angry, and was actually quite happy being in his sober head. So it didn't make any sense. Rob was struggling with why he drank.

A habit?

Perhaps it was just a habit? Alcohol is so ingrained into our society that those who do not drink are often classed as outsiders. Rob knew it would be difficult to get through the celebratory events in his life without it. Luckily he was married so he wouldn't have to make his excuses when the champagne was opened – but his three stepchildren's weddings were another question, along with all the anniversaries for ever more. He wondered what he would order in the pub rather than his beloved Guinness? He wondered how he would feel as Annabel savoured their favourite full-bodied Chilean merlot while he watched on? What Rob knew for sure now was that, as in his previous addictions, he had to stop partaking completely. It just wasn't possible for him to cut down. This was a lifestyle change and he was ready.

He thought back to last night and couldn't even remember getting home. The kids were all out at sleepovers and Annabel and he had been invited to a neighbour's dinner party. The wine had started flowing at 8pm and continued until around 3am when they had switched to shots. His stomach turned just thinking about it, and churned further with the taste that vodka always gave him the day after, which lingered on his breath. They'd had a few hours sleep when the first of the children had been dropped off on Sunday morning and Rob couldn't even stomach breakfast he felt so awful. He'd heard many times that an addict has to reach rock bottom before starting the long ascent back to sanity, and this was definitely one of those rolling around at the bottom of the pit moments. He'd been here so many times before, though, and always vowed it would never happen again, but it always did. He felt like he was trapped on a hamster wheel, going around the same feelings, patterns and emotions as the last time, the time before, and the time before that. All of a sudden he saw just how stupid it was. He didn't want to despise himself any longer, and as he thought back to last night he dreaded to think what he said to their friends, he had no recollection.

It was embarrassing not to be able to remember and he had a tight knot of dread as he ran through the little he did remember.

The whole of Sunday was complete torture and Rob felt awful that what should be quality time with the kids was reduced to snapping at them or ignoring them completely and numbly watching rubbish TV.

Monday morning couldn't come quick enough and as the alcohol gradually departed from Rob's body, he felt his mood and body lighten. He was himself again thank god. It was such a relief to not feel like shit and Rob once again felt a surge of motivation to never feel like that again.

Come on man, you can do this!

Wednesday evening was the first test of his resolve. Annabel had opened a bottle of red and was happily drinking and cooking dinner. To Rob's surprise it didn't bother him at all and he felt extremely satisfied (and maybe a little smug) with his orange squash.

Friday he bailed out of going to the pub with the boys as he didn't feel ready to put himself through that, so instead he took Annabel to the cinema where they indulged in pick-a-mix, popcorn and cola. Annabel didn't mention the fact that they'd not gone to the cinema in about three years because Rob hated going, and he guessed she was being silently supportive of his no-alcohol plans.

Saturday was spent mildly anxious about not drinking that evening, and much worse, not drinking the following day with Sunday dinner. There was nowhere he could hide, and no cunning plan he could muster to get out of that one!

As it happened Saturday night passed quite easily, but Sunday was a struggle. Annabel's Dad came over for dinner as usual and the pair of them polished off a good Pinot Noir. He on the other hand pushed the boat out for him and the kids and got through three bottles of Appletiser! He had to admit it tasted really good in a wine glass, and instead of spending the rest of the day crashed out on the sofa either asleep or watching TV, he got so many jobs done through the day and evening that usually would have been ignored. By 9pm on Sunday evening he felt quietly proud of himself and the inner strength he had developed. He knew the following couple of days would be fine as he didn't usually drink until Wednesday, and this coming Wednesday just happened to be his and Annabel's anniversary. They were booked into their favourite Spanish restaurant where they normally consumed two bottles of wine. He pushed it from his mind and returned to his weekend achievement and smiled.

Wednesday came and all day he looked forward to eating tapas that night. They were regulars at Casa Lua and Peta the waitress came straight over.

"Evening guys" she said in her strong New Zealand accent.

"Hiya, Peta" they both chorused.

"Shall I bring over a bottle of Rioja?" it wasn't even a question, more a statement. In the hundred times they had eaten there they always had a bottle of Rioja to get the evening going.

"Well actually I'm not drinking tonight" Rob confessed.

"Really!" even Annabel was surprised.

"Why on earth not?" asked Peta.

"Just having a little break from drinking, that's all" he replied.

"I'm still going to have the wine, please, Peta." Annabel then asked Rob, "Is that OK?"

"Of course it is" he said "Enjoy!"

"What will you be drinking, Rob?" asked Peta.

"I'll have a bottle of water please," he answered.

"OK" said Peta, "One bottle of Rioja with one glass and a bottle of water with two glasses," and she walked off.

In all honesty Rob had not said to Annabel that he was never drinking again. She had heard him say that so many times before, and he had never followed through. This time, however, it felt different. He felt stronger and more sure in himself that this was what he wanted, and he was going to show Annabel this through his actions rather than his words.

It was such a massive step, and he felt something so unusual as for the first time he really tasted his tapas without alcohol clouding his mind or his taste buds. The food was delicious and he was actually really enjoying himself. Why was he so surprised?

Rob suddenly became very aware of the noise level in the restaurant rising as everyone's intoxication rose too. The lights were suddenly dimmed and a birthday cake was produced to the table by the window. He had not really noticed before how noisy the restaurant could get. Annabel downed the last glass from the bottle as they shared a cheeseboard.

Later on when tucked up in bed and just before yet another sound night's sleep, Rob reflected on the evening and couldn't get the smug smile off his face. Annabel was snoring next to him, but he knew that deep sleep was very close.

The next morning he noticed his jeans were a bit loose and jumped onto the scales. He had lost four pounds since the last time he weighed himself, which was around the time of his last drink. He couldn't believe how many positive effects there were to not drinking. He was also feeling a lot happier as well as more focused. He was loving it.

There were no plans for the weekend, but the following weekend they'd been invited to a fortieth birthday party about 25 miles away. Rob's initial response was to find a nearby hotel so that they could both drink and not worry about who was driving and was busy making phone calls and getting prices, when an idea struck him: he could drive and save them at least £100!

He laughed to himself as he noticed the subtle shifts in how he was thinking. Not only was he now able to do things that he couldn't do before, but for the first time he was comfortable planning an event in the future that he would be sober at.

It was a huge step.

Crashing off the wagon

Two steps forward, and two steps back, Rob reasoned to himself. He was nursing a hangover and feeling very disappointed in himself. He had felt so sure that he'd kicked it, then succumbed to that evil Chilean Merlot on Sunday lunchtime. One bottle had turned into three somehow over the course of the afternoon and evening, and his body and mind was now suffering relentlessly.

He didn't understand why he did something that he didn't actually want to do, when no one was forcing him or egging him on. He was a grown man, for God's sake, so why couldn't he just keep to his word? It was so frustrating.

As the week wore on he found himself drinking more than he usually would, every available opportunity in fact. This went on for the next month when Rob suddenly realised he had slipped into his do-it-to-the-extreme-now-you're-off-the-wagon thing. He thought back to his smoking days and he had done the exact same thing with that addiction too. Blimey, he really was chasing his tail.

The realisation of this pattern frustrated him all the more, if he could see what he was doing why couldn't he work out why he was doing it?

A cry for help

Rob was low, depressed, anxious, deflated, sad, angry and now drinking every day. It was like it was consuming him and right now he was definitely losing the battle. He hated that the children only ever saw him drunk, and felt lost in the cycle of intoxication, hangover, and subsequent depression.

He started to get some nasty headaches that he couldn't shift and ended up at his doctor's. He'd always had a great relationship with his GP and suddenly found himself telling this man about his drink problem.

"It's eating me up, and I can't seem to control it."

"Well, I can see that you think it's a problem, so let's have a look at what your options are."

His doctor was reassuring and calm, and they talked through the various support groups that were out there.

"I think I'd feel most comfortable talking to someone one to one rather than going to AA," Rob decided.

"Well, if that is the right decision for you, then I can refer you to our local counselling service." Dr Davies wrote down a phone number for Rob to call, which he did as soon as he got home before he changed his mind. He made an appointment and already felt a tad brighter.

My addictive patterns are driving me crazy

Rob sat down opposite Tali and started to tell her about his trail of addictions to cocaine, cigarettes and alcohol (among other things) that spanned the last 20 years.

Tali let him talk for most of the first session and it was interesting to see the last 20 years hanging out on a line for him to see collectively rather than focusing on just one area. He already knew he played out patterns of behaviour over and over again, but talking it all through in such detail in one session had an extraordinary affect on him.

Tali told him that perhaps he was being too hard on himself and that everyone struggling with an addiction was going to have some rough moments.

His mood lifted slightly through the week as he reflected on the first session and tried to not be too tough on himself when he had a glass of wine or two, or three...

As the weeks passed Rob found himself really looking forward to his counselling sessions, and the clarity it was bringing to his situation. He was surprised initially that there were other problematic areas of his life that Tali and he talked about, and that everything was subtly linked. He felt his head lighten and miraculously the headaches that he'd originally visited his GP about vanished.

Gradually the cloudy sky started to open up and show glimpses of blue, and sometimes even dazzling sunlight would shine through. Rob was feeling stronger as he began to understand himself better, and the shards of sunlight in his mind ignited his motivation to help himself.

After all the addictions that he had fought and won before, Rob knew that he couldn't force himself to stop drinking. It had to come naturally, when he was truly ready. The many times he had abstained before always led to much heavier bouts of drinking because he had been craving the drug for the whole of the restrained period.

He knew that if he tried to stop before he was ready he was in for more disappointment, so he decided to keep drinking while the counselling sessions seemed to be opening him up to a deeper part of himself. He would know when the time was right.

The time is right now

The months chugged onwards and the weekly sessions continued. Rob noticed that his drinking had suddenly got heavier in the past week and realised another of his habitual patterns was being played out.

It seemed that before he was able to let go of an addiction, Rob had to overload himself with it first. He'd done this with smoking to the point of throwing the poison up, and now he was doing the same with booze. He was drinking even on days that he normally didn't, and to the extreme too.

Once he realised, Rob also started to experience excitement that he actually felt ready to cease drinking!

It was mid-week so Rob decided that the following Monday was going to be the day. He drunk himself stupid all weekend and on Tali's advice started to write a journal of his feelings.

Diary entry Friday 18th November:
"Something has clicked in my head. I've been here before so many times with my other addictions, which I have successfully

overcome, that it seems very obvious that I can now apply the same effort, rules and resolve that I have used many times before.

When I stopped smoking it took some time to move past the urge to smoke, and I trained myself into new habits. I drink habitually so the first few times I'm in those situations are going to be strange, different and maybe even hard, but I am going to overcome them and make new habits. Even if it's hard tonight when we're out and I'm the only one not drinking. But that will become my new habit. And being sober will become my new habit. Watch this space!"

Saturday 19th November:
"It was easy! Oh my God! But I do actually feel different, this time I feel very sure that I am finally ready to let go of the feeling of intoxication. What I've realised is that I like myself a lot more when I'm sober, so what is the point of continually obliterating the real me? OK, I may have problems in my life, but who doesn't? ... and those problems are still going to be there if I drink myself to the point of blacking out, and will actually seem even worse with a horrific hangover in the morning.

I had a lovely evening last night and there was not one second that 'the urge' tried to push me off course. In fact, I can imagine that 'the urge' looks like a red angry monster inside me, and every time I do not have a drink I am diminishing 'the urge's' power over me. It is like a see-saw of power, and every day that I would normally have a drink and don't, and create a new sober habit for myself, the seesaw swings further in my direction."

Chapter One

Sunday 20th November:
"Today has passed alcohol free without a single urge. The red monster inside me has been completely silent today even though everyone around me has been drinking wine with Sunday dinner.

I feel great. Clear-headed, happy and sober! I can definitely get used to feeling like this, having my Sundays and life back. It's now seven alcohol free days, and just the beginning of my sober future."

Saturday 3rd December:
"Twenty days of not drinking now and I feel amazing. The urge to drink has disappeared completely! I feel like someone has released me from prison, I am free.

The red monster seems to have relinquished power, and rears his ugly head now only briefly when I am triggered. What is different is this now only happens for a few seconds, rather than minutes, and I can easily overcome it.

The triggers are times, places and people. I know that every time I overcome one of these I am creating new positive habits."

Monday 12th December:
"One month today! Wow! I cannot believe how amazing I feel, and that I do not feel like I am depriving myself at all. I do not want to drink is the simple fact of the matter. I'm looking forward to my first ever sober Christmas and bringing in the New Year sober too. Life is exciting, and I'm really proud of myself."

Progress

Rob felt great each week that he saw Tali and could tell her he had still not had a drink. He felt that now that issue had been dealt with, he was ready to look at other areas of his life with equal gusto.

A huge weight had been lifted, one that had been dragging Rob down for years, and he felt excited, proud, and hopeful for the future.

He felt that something had shifted in his mind that was not about to shift back again, it was one-way traffic.

Now the thought of getting drunk seemed ridiculous and he couldn't believe how his view of it had changed in just a few months. In fact, he was disgusted with the thought of drinking to the same degree as he now hated smoking! Already he felt great distance between him and it, and that was just fine.

Imaginary friends

In their next session Tali was digging around in Rob's past for clues as to where Rob's compulsion to get high was coming from, when they stumbled upon his childhood behaviour.

Reflectively he began to describe that as the older brother Rob had been the one to push boundaries and break the rules, whilst his younger brother toed the line and took more of a backseat. He said he remembered doing something naughty himself and blaming it on his brother, "It was him, not me!" he'd lie to his parents.

Rob then went on to describe his two imaginary friends, big Rob and little Rob. Big Rob was very naughty and little Rob was very good.

Tali was smiling and asked Rob if he still had an element of big Rob and little Rob now.

He laughed as he seriously considered this, "Does this make me mad?!"

"No, but maybe when you're caught up in an addiction you have these two voices pulling you in different directions." Tali paused, swallowed, and continued, "You have little Rob, the voice of reason guiding you away from your addiction, and big Rob coaxing you further down the destructive route. I think you have been aware of these two aspects of yourself from early childhood, Rob."

He was deep in his thoughts, remembering as far back as his memories would go, of doing something that he knew he shouldn't be doing but doing it anyway. Rob walked back to his car in a daze. He loved how his counselling sessions made him really think about, and become accountable for, his actions. He was understanding himself and why he did things a lot more now with the help of Tali.

Liberation

For Rob the counselling sessions were an opportunity to exhibit his problems and issues in a gallery and stand back to view and discuss each one in detail with an expert. By displaying and inspecting them they lost a great deal of their power over him, as they were now external and not eating him up inside any longer. Also his mind had been freed up now that he was not constantly stressing about alcohol. In fact, for the past 20 years he had worked through his addictions one by one and been absolutely obsessed about each one. They had filled his head, allowing no time or effort for anything else. Now they were all gone and this was a completely new feeling for Rob. He'd constantly moved to the next destructive poison in his life, but now he was rid of them all.

He was quite literally a liberated man and he had not

expected just quite how deeply, and on so many levels, he was going to feel different. To be no longer bound by a substance was something that Rob had not before experienced as an adult.

The effect was he felt stronger mentally and physically, and if he only knew what he knew now he would have done it all so much sooner! But he understood that he had conquered each addiction when he was ready and that was all anyone could do. However, he truly believed that anyone who could step outside of their addiction for just three weeks would see amazing benefit and stand a good chance of succeeding.

He felt freer than he'd ever felt before by having this new perspective, and knew this was what he had longed for for the last few years. In fact, he was now really enjoying life, it had become lighter and less serious and Rob's mind now rested on how he was going to maintain feeling so good about himself.

Rob asked Tali at their next session: "I feel great, Tali, on top of the world even, but I'm worried about losing this feeling."

"Just take one day at a time Rob and try not to stress yourself out, you're doing so well."

"But what happens if I wake up one day and want a drink? I keep dreaming that I get really drunk, and wake up not knowing if it's actually happened or not and panic that it is true!"

"Please stop worrying, Rob, it is very common to have these dreams, and is a good indication of how seriously you want to not drink."

"I just feel like there's a big gaping hole where my addictions used to be which needs to be occupied by something more helpful and positive."

"Have you ever tried meditation, Rob?"

"No, I haven't."

"It's just that I know a very lovely local teacher who says that meditation stabilises the mind and makes it stronger. It's possible that it may help you at this stage, and you don't really have anything to lose by trying."

Rob took the details of the teacher home with him and did some research online. Jo was indeed very local to him and her Thursday evening class suited his schedule. He emailed her and booked himself into the following weeks class. He'd never done anything like it before but was willing to see if his mind felt more stable through meditation.

Addicted to meditation

The class was indeed very calming the following Thursday evening, and Rob was surprised at how quickly the 30 minutes passed by.

"Everyone says that!" said Jo with a smile.

"I'd like to continue coming if that's OK?" Rob said, hopefully.

"Of course, you are very welcome."

Rob became a regular and practised a few minutes at home everyday also. He definitely felt less stressed and started to stop worrying all the time as he began to realise that all this worrying was getting him nowhere. His mind did indeed settle and stabilise and perhaps, he admitted, he had got a little addicted to meditation!

The practice taught him to let go of everything, and allow his mind to rest. This concept supported how he was feeling now his addictions were at bay, and he became more and more adjusted to feeling balanced, calm and in control.

These were all emotions he'd never experienced before and the meditation was like a friend that he would go and visit everyday, and share his newfound happiness with.

The empty hole that his addictions had left behind had been more than filled by his meditation practice, and everyone in his life could notice the positive changes in him.

Fortieth birthday

Rob was looking forward to turning 40 in a few months. He had spent the whole of his twenties partying and taking illegal drugs, the whole of his thirties drunk, and was now ready to start his forties sober. He felt happier and healthier than he'd ever felt before, even if his stepchildren thought he was *really* old!

He was planning a big party, and wanted everyone to know how great it was to be sober.

Rob's mind travelled back through his career of addictions, and he thought meditation was absolutely the most positive addiction of all. When Jo told the group about her upcoming retreat she was leading in Norfolk, Rob jumped at the chance of attending. He was definitely ready to take his practice to the next level and spend a whole weekend in contemplation.

Chapter Two

Sam

I'm Sick of Walking on Eggshells

"Beneath the scabs of our wounds are where the sites of new growth can be found."
Unknown

Sam was unhappy and knew there was more for her beyond the confines of her relationship with Bobby, but why did she stay? It seemed that she asked this same question to herself everyday but never got any nearer to decisive action. They had been together for 10 years and in her heart she knew she had been unhappy for 9 of them. It seemed so silly to know all of this but to lack the courage to do anything about it.

Bobby was such a good man deep down, but just found it hard to show it. Actually if Sam was completely honest with herself he could show it to everyone else apart from her. They had managed to get themselves wound up into a tight ball of bitterness, resentment and unhappiness. It was a constant fight and Sam felt she had to walk on eggshells probably about 90% of the time, as Bobby was untrusting, jealous and possessive.

Bobby fell in love with a confident, popular, attractive,

fun-loving girl but year after year clipped away at her wings, stopped her from seeing her friends, until she was a shadow of her former self. In fact her friends had stopped even asking her out as she was never allowed and if she did it caused huge problems. She thought back to the last time she had managed to see her friends...

Was it worth it?

Sam loved going out, drinking, dancing and having fun. She really knew how to enjoy herself given half the chance! It was a great night of catching up, so many laughs and some dancing too. Then it was time to go home and a sinking feeling seemed to swallow Sam up, as she knew Bobby would be difficult, and she so wished things could be different. She tiptoed up the stairs and let herself in as quietly as she could, ensuring the door latch didn't spring up and wake him as all was dark in their flat. She checked her watch, 1.13am, "Not too late," she thought to herself as she undressed and slipped into bed next to Bobby. He was in a deep sleep and didn't move a millimetre as she snuggled up to him.

The next morning they slept in as it was Sunday and Sam noticed that Bobby was awake when she opened her eyes.

"Morning," she said.

Silence.

"Morning, Bobby," she repeated.

Nothing!

Bobby then got out of bed and walked out of the bedroom without even looking at her, and he was mad!

Sam lay there completely confused as to what was going on. Had she missed something? She walked into the kitchen where Bobby was making coffee for himself and asked, "Are you mad at me babe?"

He glared at her.

"If I've done something wrong you could at least tell me what it is?" she tried desperately, but it was like drawing blood from a stone.

Bobby took his coffee into the living room, lit a cigarette, and turned the news on, still ignoring her.

Sam spun around and made her way into the bathroom where she closed the door and collapsed in a heap on the floor. Tears ran down her cheeks and she sobbed quietly.

It was always like this, she wasn't really surprised. Bobby would be mad all day and she'd be lucky to get one word out of him and for what? She'd done nothing wrong!

Sam showered and looked in the mirror as she dried herself off. Sam's blue eyes were like tiny pinpricks hidden inside huge red puffy lids. Her skin was sensitive and always looked awful after a bout of crying, and she also had a dusting of zits around her nose and chin. As she inspected her auburn curls she found a couple of grey hairs and thought how unfair it was to have both spots and grey hairs. Surely if you were old enough for one you were too old for the other? She was 31 and could feel changes happening in her body and to her looks. Wrinkles were forming on her face, and her metabolism was definitely slowing down causing her waistline to expand. Her diet hadn't changed so she put it down to the ageing process. Sam applied some mascara to try mask her bulbous eyes, brushed her hair and thought how awful she looked and felt. Finally she was ready to leave the peaceful sanctuary of the bathroom. The moment she walked out she could feel the angry air and as Bobby looked up in her direction he glared at her. He was so angry.

She dressed and picked up the car keys.

"I'm going to the supermarket" she informed him. She simply had to get out of that hateful environment. Bobby continued to ignore her, but then shouted, "Get me some cigarettes," just as she shut the door.

Sam took her time wandering up and down the isles, but had to be careful not to put too much in her trolley. Bobby got very vocal when she spent too much money, but it was really good to get out of the flat. How sad was it to enjoy Tesco so much. God she was unhappy.

Why does he have to be such an arsehole?

As she climbed the stairs with the heavy bags of shopping, Bobby silently started to help her. He seemed to have calmed down a bit, but was still not speaking.

She was used to it of course, and knew the remainder of the day would be spent in front of the telly with the only communication between them being about what to watch.

Again Sam questioned herself as to why she put up with this ridiculous behaviour.

"I love him," she said in her head.

"But this is not normal behaviour between two people who love each other," another voice interjected.

"I love him" there was that pathetic voice again.

"Is that enough, though?" came reason's voice.

This conversation whirled around in her head as she started to prepare Sunday roast. Bobby was laid out on the sofa happily watching Arsenal defeat Manchester United. The sting had definitely been taken out of his mood but he had still not spoken a word to her.

She peeled the potatoes, started to boil them and put a large piece of lamb in the oven.

"Where did you go last night?" Bobby had come into the kitchen, and was all of a sudden showing some interest in her.

"You know, babe, I went to the Castle in Woodford with the girls," she replied.

"But you didn't get in til three," his tone of voice was rough and unpleasant.

"Actually, Bobs, it was just after one cos I looked at my watch, and anyway the pub shuts at 12.30 and I drove back," she found herself having to explain.

"Well *actually* I know it was three because I was awake," accused Bobby.

"Why on earth are we having this conversation? Does it even matter what time I come home?! I am a grown woman after all, and I hardly *ever* go out!" shouted Sam.

"What matters is that if you can so easily lie about what time you got in, what else are you lying about? Maybe you were out with another man!"

Bobby had so much hate in his voice, and over the years he had accused her so many times of cheating. In fact he'd accused her of sleeping with all his friends.

Sam had never cheated in the whole 10 years of them being together, but sometimes she wondered why not? She got accused anyway!

They continued to argue in the kitchen as the dinner was prepared, and sat in silence at the table as they ate. Sam usually loved her roast lamb dinner but today all she could taste was anger, resentment and hatred, which filled the food and the flat.

She pushed her plate away and went into the bedroom and lay on the bed.

This had happened so many times before, every time she went out in fact, which is why it was easier to not go out with her friends (whom Bobby seemed to hate) and keep the peace.

They would live in virtual silence for the next few days, until Bobby decided he was no longer angry. Sam knew she had to ride it out and wait for his anger to simmer and eventually subside, but she hated living like this and knew she had to do something about it. But she just didn't know what or how, and why couldn't he have just said: "Did you have a nice night out with your friends?"

That was the worst apology ever

As predicted, they spoke about five words to each other that week so Sam was extremely surprised when she walked through the door on Thursday to find a beautiful meal cooked for her by Bobby. They sat down to eat and chatted about their days at work as if nothing had happened. There was no mention of the weekend's argument or the problems they faced in their relationship. Once again it was brushed under the carpet and seemingly forgotten.

Unfortunately, when you sweep emotions under the carpet they fester and decay, maturing over time and becoming even more problematic.

Sam was happy that the air was clear once again, but deep within her heart yet another disappointment had been stored where all the other arguments, bitter words and unhappiness were housed.

She felt weak to just let it go, but didn't have the energy to keep the argument going.

Is he even capable of treating me right?

One morning Bobby woke up and told Sam how much he loved her. What a wonderful start to the day! Sam put all her negative emotions toward him aside and stupidly believed that everything was OK again.

She floated off to work and imagined all day what a wonderful life they were going to have together.

Chapter Two

It lasted all of six days, but Sam milked Bobby's good mood for all it was worth. Nice words came out of his mouth and he was kind and considerate towards her.

On the Saturday Sam spent the whole day tidying, washing, cleaning, dusting, and sorting. She enjoyed getting their home organised and her mood was high. She heard Bobby's key in the door and rushed over to greet him. He was still in a good mood and bent down to kiss her. She looked into his piercing blue eyes and thought how much she loved him. She then ran a hand over his clean-shaven head and across the ear occupied by a gold stud. She asked him about his day on the building site, and he asked about hers.

"Well, I can see you've been busy," he said jovially.

"The whole flat is spotless!" Sam was proud.

They talked for a few more minutes then Bobby asked: "Did you pick up the dry cleaning?"

"Oops," said Sam, "I forgot. I was so engrossed in getting the flat tidy I've not even been out."

"I don't believe you!" Bobby spat. "I needed my shirt this weekend. You're so selfish, you only think of yourself!"

He was fuming and red in the face as he shouted at her.

As Sam sat down, it was like her body folded into a dejected heap. How could she have been so stupid as to think that Bobby had changed and was now going to treat her well. She felt like a fool. It always amazed her that he could snap so easily, over the smallest thing. One minute absolutely fine, the next a bundle of simmering anger.

She couldn't pretend anymore that there was nothing wrong between them, and she knew she had to do something, but she loved him and wanted it to work so much, why didn't he? It was horribly painful.

Sam spent the night watching TV in their bedroom, while Bobby stayed in the living room. They couldn't bear to even be in the same room together, each harbouring angry thoughts about the other. This was not how Sam imagined the love of her life should treat her, so she sulked and felt sorry for herself all night. It seemed that she cried pretty much everyday about this hopeless relationship, but felt weak and powerless to make the changes that were called for.

The thought of breaking up was too much to bear as they had been through so much together, *surely he could change?*

It's wonderful to have fabulous friends

The following weekend Sam went out to lunch with some of her closest friends and sister. Lunch dates were much safer than going out in the evening, causing far fewer arguments with Bobby.

Sam was obviously really down and her girlfriends picked up on this immediately.

"If you ever need to, you can crash at mine," Sally was saying.

"Yeah and at mine" Louise agreed.

"And at mine," Sam's sister, George offered.

"I don't think it's that bad," Sam was absolutely not ready to give up on Bobby and stormed off to the toilet.

"Oh dear," Louise said to the other girls, "we need to tread carefully, she's obviously not ready for that conversation yet."

"No, but it's good that it's been said, so that she knows she has options when the time is right," Al said.

"The thing is she has to make that decision herself in her own time" George continued. "If she makes it too early, then she'll just go back to him or straight into the arms of someone equally controlling."

"Let's just support her however she needs it," Al said, and the others all agreed.

Sam came back in and had big red swollen eyes from crying. "I'm a mess" she said.

"We are all here for you, no matter what" Sally assured her.

"All I want is for us to make each other happy, why can't he be nice to me?" Sam questioned.

The girls looked at each other, what could they say? None of them liked Bobby as he controlled their friend and make her desperately unhappy. They all agreed that when Sam and Bobby were together Sam was half the girl she was when with her friends. It was like she wasn't allowed to be the fun-loving, vivacious, confident, funny girl she really was. He was an oppressor and a manipulative one at that.

"Why is this happening to me?" Sam cried some more into her nachos and coffee.

The most awful two hours of her life

She was thick within a victim role, and felt powerless in the situation. It was like she was trapped and had no way out. She knew he was a good person deep down, *so why couldn't he show her that?*

Sam and Bobby lived in a rented flat, and although their landlady hated dogs, she had allowed them to move Foxy Lady in. She was Bobby's dog and he'd always promised Sam that he'd take care of her (Sam was a cat lover).

Unfortunately Foxy had got into the habit of doing her doggy business on the large terrace adjoining their flat. Bobby wasn't great at clearing up the poo as he'd promised, and it was usually left to Sam to discard of before their landlady saw it, as she would go ballistic.

Sam was alone when the doorbell went and found her irate landlady standing there with fire in her eyes.

"There is dog shit everywhere on the terrace. It is absolutely disgusting! I want you out of this flat."

"Please Lynda, give me a chance. I know it's disgusting but I won't let it happen again. I'll clear it up immediately" Sam begged.

Lynda paused as she thought about the right course of action. Then she decided: "OK, but this is a warning. This happens again, and you and your filthy dog are out." She turned on her heel and stomped off.

"Thank you" Sam weakly called after her and closed the door.

She was a tiny bit pissed off with Bobby because she'd asked him to move the mess, but annoyed with herself mainly for allowing it to get so bad.

That night they were out with friends, and Sam didn't immediately tell Bobby about what had happened as she had a sinking feeling he would kick off. It seemed the slightest problem these days was magnified into a huge argument.

They chatted for a while, then Sam gingerly gave an account of the exchange with their landlady. She didn't accuse him or tell him she thought it was his fault, just the simple fact that they had nearly got kicked out. Bobby immediately got really defensive and said, "I don't care," before walking off. Sam was crushed.

They sat in different areas of the bar for a while, then once Sam had calmed down a bit herself she came over and sat down next to Bobby. He got up and sat down on another chair, all the while holding a conversation with his friend.

This happened three or four times, Sam following Bobby around like a puppy, with him blatantly trying to get away from her.

It was the most awful two hours of her life. She watched as he laughed and joked with his friends, then scowl at her and move away when she approached. She was so embarrassed and had to leave. They were pretty local, so she made an excuse of a headache and went home alone.

She cried the whole way home, and had given herself an actual headache by the time she went to bed.

When Bobby came in, she pretended to be asleep. The next morning Bobby was in the mood to argue.

"How dare you accuse me of not clearing up the shit," he said.

"No, I didn't," she replied. "I actually was very conscious of *not* accusing you." Sam continued, "I knew you'd get arsey, so I chose my words very carefully."

"I don't believe you. You did accuse me, and blame me," Bobby shouted.

"But I don't blame you," Sam said quietly. There was absolutely no point in getting in his face, he'd just get even angrier (if that was possible). "It was horrible that you said you don't care, can you apologise for saying that?" Sam so hoped he could.

"No. I don't care. You're always nagging me. Leave me alone," and with that he walked out.

I need some space away from you

Sam was left with hers and Bobby's problems again. "I cannot accept his words and actions," she thought. "I am sick of being constantly disappointed and hurt by him." She knew she had to move forward from this point, and not look back like she usually did. She had settled into a routine of letting Bobby's bad behaviour go just to keep the peace and have some lightness back. But the truth was it was eating away at her to the point that she hated herself more and more for accepting how he treated her. She didn't think she could pretend she was OK for much longer.

"He can take 'I don't care' somewhere else, to someone else. I want someone who DOES CARE and isn't afraid of showing it." She shouted to the empty flat. Foxy Lady came trotting round the corner wagging her tail and Sam sat on the floor with the dog, lost in thought.

Sam then decided she needed a break, and arranged to stay at her sister George's for a week. She could easily get to work from there, but she felt low, overcast and upset when George found her on the doorstep with a big full hold-all.

Tears were streaming down her face, and she ran straight up to the spare room. She couldn't even talk. Sam felt alone and empty, and just wanted Bobby to knock on the door and tell her it was OK, he loved her, and it was all going to be OK.

He obviously didn't and it obviously wasn't.

The next morning Sam slunk down the stairs and sat with George and her husband J for breakfast.

"Last night I cried so hard, I thought I was going to explode," she confessed. "My head is pounding, but I don't think there could possibly be any fluid left in me now for more crying."

"Why don't you phone in sick today, and have the house to yourself?" George suggested.

"That sounds like a really good idea" Sam replied.

She moped around the house all day, unable to eat, spending most of the time gazing into the garden and watching the autumn leaves tumble haphazardly in the weak sun. Sam wrote a lot of her feelings down in her journal, which she found easier than verbalising.

Diary excerpt:
"Right now I am feeling like Jekyll and Hyde. I am sliced down the middle. My heart is speaking to me but my head is saying the opposite!
Which way do I go?

Do I accept his behaviour, or do I lose everything for a dream that may not exist?

I love him with my whole heart, and he loves me with his whole heart (in his own way) and I'm not satisfied with that, it's not enough!

How ridiculous, who do I think I am?

Am I being selfish and unrealistic?

Or am I just being true to myself?

I do believe you can have anything in life if you just make it happen. So along these lines I'm not being unrealistic and I should leave Bobby and find someone who understands me, loves me, adores me, AND SHOWS IT!

But Bobby does sometimes understand me, love me and adore me (I think) he just doesn't know how to show it or express it. IS IT ENOUGH???

Who am I kidding!

Am I really going to accept second best because I'm hurting so bad?

IT'S NOT FAIR!"

She was even more confused about how she felt by the time her sister and brother-in-law came home from work, but Sam was starving now so they ordered a curry and watched America's Next Top Model on TV.

It had now been over 24 hours since Sam had seen or spoken to Bobby. There had been no big romantic gesture from him, and she couldn't hide her disappointment.

"Why doesn't he feel the same way about me?" she winged to George and J.

"You have no control over how he feels you know, you must get out of that mindset and start to think about what you need to do." George continued, "Do you think you can ever find happiness in this relationship? Can you remember feeling truly happy?"

"Well, it does seem to be a struggle most of the time, but I love him so much." Sam was really whining now.

"Well, to be honest, you are acting like a victim, when you are actually choosing to stay and, therefore, accepting his behaviour towards you."

George's words had the same affect as a slap around the face.

"Ouch," was her response.

"I'm sorry if it sounds harsh, sis, but every time you forgive his appalling words and actions, you are really saying it's OK, and, can I have some more please."

George had held her tongue for years because she did not want to alienate her sister, but now was definitely the right time to explain, as an outsider, what she saw going on. She continued, "His rude and angry behaviour isn't just going to miraculously stop."

Wow, Sam felt sick, but on some level absolutely knew and agreed that what George was saying was right.

But George couldn't stop now (maybe it was the mushroom madras that was firing her system up), and had to keep going now that the floodgate had been opened.

"You have been together for so long and by staying together and not addressing the problems, you have signalled over and over again that his bad behaviour is OK," she paused for effect. "He needs to understand the consequences of his negative behaviour, and he will never be able to do that if you continue on this horrific merry-go-round."

George then stopped, she'd said enough. It was now time for that huge information to settle and for Sam to formulate some sort of response. George only hoped she'd said enough, and the right thing, to help set her sister free.

The scales start to tip

Sam knew deep down that she was supposed to be happy, no one was meant to be miserable. But each individual has to fight for their happiness and create the right environment for it. For the past 10 years Sam knew this but couldn't apply it to her life. It was like she was engulfed in thick grey clouds that kept her held back in despair, and it was simply too hard and painful to break through to the other side where the sun was shining and happiness was waiting. Oh and she agreed with *everything* George had said that night.

She now lay in bed and listened as a train chuffed past and a couple were arguing somewhere close by. Her ears suddenly pricked up as she tuned into the angry words. Wow! That was what her and Bobby's neighbours had to put up with regularly!

Sam was thinking so much her head hurt, so she decided she needed to write something down to get a new perspective.

She started to make two lists:

Unacceptable behaviour from Bobby and from herself.

Unacceptable behaviour – Bobby

- Volatile temper
- Exploding over small things
- Making snide remarks about her friends
- Possessiveness
- Not showing genuine interest in her / being together
- Blaming others. Never seeing his part in creating problems = always her fault!
- Angry towards her all the time

Unacceptable behaviour – Sam

- Not talking to him when hurt/upset, for fear of conflict
- Feeling powerless around him
- Speaking/acting in a way I'm not feeling, so therefore not genuine

- Moulding my life around his needs and not doing what I want to do
- Giving a lot more than comes back
- Wanting to cling to him
- Ignoring nasty behaviour

There was no getting away from how lob-sided their relationship was when it was written out in this way. It was starting to sink in that this relationship might not be worth saving.

The penny finally drops

The next morning Sam phoned in sick again, but assured her boss she was feeling marginally better and would definitely be back the following day.

She felt sluggish and lethargic, and although she'd slept well, her mind was foggy and unclear. One thing was for sure, however, she knew this morning that it was over. She could not go back to Bobby.

It filled her with dread and she had no idea how she was going to do it, but something had happened overnight in her head, and there was now no going back. She had begun her journey to push through the fog and find the sunnier, happier place she knew she deserved.

It had now been one full week that she had been at George's and no word from Bobby. Every time the phone rang or the doorbell sounded she wished it was him, but to no avail, it never was. She was jumpy, unsure of herself, and still had nagging doubts about whether she was doing the right thing. But she sat tight, and kept telling herself it would get easier as time went on. George had suggested talking to a professional about how she was feeling but Sam wasn't sure she wanted to tell a complete stranger her deepest fears and insecurities.

As it happened one of her friends was seeing a life-coach and the next time she saw Louise she asked her about it.

"So what's it like opening up to a stranger, Lou?"

"It's good, actually. Weird to begin with, but you soon build up a close and trusting relationship and I always walk out feeling 10 times better than when I walked in."

It got Sam thinking so she took the name and website details from her friend and went home to investigate.

It would appear that Jo also taught yoga, which Sam wasn't interested in, and she clicked straight onto the coaching page to glean some more information.

Jo used words like 'supporting', 'guiding', and 'healing' and it did really appeal to Sam.

She needed to fill the void where her relationship to Bobby used to be, and she did need some guidance, some support and to heal.

Jo also talked about happiness coming from the inside, and Sam had spent so long wanting someone else to make her happy and being constantly disappointed and unhappy, that she wanted to learn how to find it within herself, as she had absolutely no idea.

Sam had a good feeling about it so she sent Jo an email there and then requesting a meeting.

Jo immediately got in touch and their first session was booked for later on in the week. Sam was reassured that she did not need to commit to any more sessions if she thought coaching was not for her. Jo said it was important for Sam to feel comfortable and that she was in the right place.

How can I tell a complete stranger everything?

Over the years Sam had been embarrassed for people to know the extent of the problems between Bobby and herself, and had never told anyone everything. The thought of this now was terrifying but she was willing to see if it helped.

Sam pensively relayed her relationship situation at length and immediately Jo reassured Sam that she had done the right thing in leaving Bobby if he made her feel so unhappy. With that Sam broke. To hear those words from her sister and now a professional made it all so final and complete. She would be such a fool to go back to him now.

Over the pursuing weeks Sam told Jo everything and, unbelievably, it felt amazing to offload all her problems in one go!

She now understood better how unhealthy and co-dependent the relationship was and soon she was paving the way for a longer stay at her sister's. George was, in fact, over the moon that her sister was staying longer and seemed to be finding a way to extract herself out of a living nightmare.

The tables have turned

Now when the phone rang, or doorbell sounded, Sam wished desperately that it *wasn't* Bobby. She was not yet ready for that conversation, and needed some more time to compose herself.

Over the subsequent weeks and months, Sam avoided all contact with Bobby and continued with her weekly coaching sessions.

One day, Jo was asking her why she sometimes felt like she wanted Bobby back.

"Security," answered Sam.

"OK, but does he really give you security?"

Sam thought long and hard.

"… just that he's there, really, and I'm not on my own."

"OK, so what is it that you feel is missing without him?" Jo probed.

"Being loved, adored and looked after," Sam said wistfully.

"OK, and does Bobby make you feel loved, adored and looked after?"

Sam laughed, "No, he doesn't!"

"Right, so you are perhaps longing for and missing something that is not even there?" Jo continued. "Would that be fair to say?"

Sam paused and a new level of understanding opened up to her.

"I am beginning to accept that he cannot make me happy, or provide me with what I need in a relationship. He's not interested in my interests, is not considerate, and not at all understanding. He doesn't take responsibility for his life or his actions, moods, or anger. I've spent ten years hoping that everything will work out OK, that he'll change and love me the way I deserve. Now I realise that that is never going to happen as I am not prepared to spend another ten years waiting! No way! So I am taking responsibility for my life and letting this relationship go."

"Wow!" Jo congratulated her.

"I think I'm just afraid of the unknown. Of being alone. I've never been on my own. I went from one relationship to another before Bobby and then the last ten years with him. It feels really, really scary to be out there all alone." It was hard for Sam to admit.

"But you're not alone, Sam. You have a strong support network around you, and once you start to get used to your new freedom, you will thrive, I just know it!"

Sam's coach was very sweet and she was so glad she'd taken that step and asked for help when she really needed it.

The shit hits the fan

Bobby did not take the news well. He must have seen it coming surely? Sam had been at George and J's for ten weeks now and not spoken to him once. Messages had been relayed to him via various people that she needed some time to think. Bobby must have thought she would come around in the end, because when she was finally ready to invite him over to her sister's (she couldn't bear to go to their flat, as she knew she'd feel weaker there) he went mad.

"You're coming home with me now!" he shouted.

Sam just sat there and didn't say another word. She'd said her well rehearsed piece, it was over, and she was not about to have yet another pointless argument with Bobby. *That part of her life was over.*

"Come on, get your stuff together, babe, let's go" he was still shouting in one last final stand.

She was sitting there with tears rolling down her cheeks and shaking her head.

Bobby was obviously in shock. He had called the shots for ten years, and was now having a tantrum like an eight year old who'd been denied the Xbox game he wanted.

"Now!" he pointed to the door.

She shook her head and stayed where she was.

"I hate you so much, Sam, and I never want to lay eyes on you again!" With that he stormed out, and immediate peace fell in the room, and in Sam's mind.

She started to laugh uncontrollably at how stupid he had sounded shouting at her in that fashion, as if she was going to say 'Oh, OK then,' and trot after him.

No one is ever going to speak to me like that again

Then it hit her. That *was* exactly what she had been doing over and over again during the last ten years. It was *she* who had changed her behaviour in the last few months, not him. No wonder he had been surprised!

She got up and opened a bottle of wine, took it and a glass over to the sofa, and sat in deep silent reflective thought. George and J had made themselves scarce and weren't due back for another hour or so.

It was perfect. She had done it. She was sad for the loss of her partner and knew the next few months would be tough, but also felt a huge weight had been lifted.

"No one is ever going to speak to me like that ever again."

She said the words out loud, and knew they were the truth. They were soothing words that held her in a comforting embrace.

It was late when George and J came home and Sam was sitting in the dark.

"How'd it go?" her sister asked.

"Really well. He shouted and told me he hated me. It went just as I thought it would!"

"And how do you feel?" J asked.

"Relieved, sad, free, happy, empty, alone…" Sam trailed off.

"Well, all those emotions are good, healthy and normal!" George continued, "Any wine left?"

Starting over

Sam collected her belongings from the flat over the next week when she knew Bobby would be at work. There was no point in seeing him again as it was just too stressful. There was no going back now. Saying goodbye to the flat she'd lived in for years, Foxy Lady, and the happy memories was hard enough.

She stored her stuff in George and J's basement, and set about looking for a flat to rent. It didn't take long, and she was soon in her own space. This was to be a place of care and consideration, with no shouting tolerated.

It was time to be alone, to get to know herself with no one else in the picture. Sam felt hopeful as she reached for her glass of wine.

Baby steps

The first few months were busy adopting her new routine, and then she started to actually enjoy her own company for the first time ever. She could watch what she wanted on TV, eat when and what she wanted, and had the full support of her friends and family when she had her wobbly moments (and there were a few).

She had thought she was going to feel lonely, and was surprised to find out that what she actually felt was very peaceful. She enjoyed the silence after being around so much shouting for so many years. The shouting had become her reality and now that it was gone a whole new world of tranquillity had opened up and settled in. Sam wore harmony like a blanket and it reached all corners of her life, and took the edge off her raw pain.

When the pangs of loneliness descended she reminded herself what it felt like to be oppressed and not have a voice. It was hard but she absolutely knew she was doing the right thing. Her clipped wings were slowly growing back and she was now looking forward to the future. Sam was back in control and had forgotten how great that felt.

Now she could let her mind be free and not constantly have to worry about what Bobby's reaction to every little thing might be. She hadn't realised how much she'd been analysing *everything* into two lists: what Bobby would approve of and therefore she could bring up, and what she thought Bobby would not approve of and she therefore felt that she had to hide or suppress.

Sam thought back to the previous Christmas and the photos of her work party. She'd been quite drunk and taken loads of photos. When the photos had been developed Sam was excited to look through them, and there were some classics! Then a photo popped out of Sam with a group of boys and her mood dropped, she would not be able to show that one to Bobby as he'd go mad.

It had become normal behaviour to hide things from her partner that she knew would cause problems. For example: if she was meeting a male friend she'd lie and say that they were female, or if she spent quite a lot of money on clothing she would halve the total to cushion the blow (not that she ever bought much). Life was already so volatile that Sam felt she had to do anything she could to make it easier for herself.

The beginning of the rest of my life

It was like getting to know herself all over again. She'd changed and adapted so much to appease Bobby that she'd got lost somewhere between being accused of sleeping with his best friend, and being a selfish cow for doing the housework rather than iron his shirt. Sam had forgotten what she truly liked to do, liked to eat, and like to listen to. The pain of the break-up was subsiding, and Sam was waking up once more. She felt happier everyday. Now Sam was getting used to *not* bending the truth or having to explain herself to anyone. Such a weight had been lifted and as time went by she realised that there had been *no* shouting in her life for months (then years).

Then came the subject of dating again. She'd been with the same man for ten years and couldn't wait to sample someone new, how exciting!

Sam was very clear, however, not to get into a serious relationship yet. She was still healing and getting to know herself as an individual, and was definitely not ready to bring someone else into that equation.

Her new-found freedom brought a smile to Sam's lips and she thought back to how she felt in the confines of her old relationship. If only she had known how free she could feel, she would have done this years ago. Sam was pleased that she had listened to her head and believed that there was something better out there. She had not been truly living for the past ten years, *she had been surviving*.

Sam also trusted the voice in her heart that assured her that there was someone out there for her who would understand and support her totally, and looked forward to the day that that person came into her life.

Soon Sam thought she might be up for a holiday alone, and started searching the internet for something that appealed.

She stumbled upon a photography weekend, walking weekend, and then a picture of Jo, her coach and mentor popped up! Jo held weekend retreats that included coaching along with yoga and meditation, in the comfort of a gorgeous house. It was perfect. She always felt so uplifted after just one hour of coaching, so Sam knew that a whole weekend was going to be bliss. She brought it up in their next coaching session, "I'm really interested in coming to one of your retreats Jo but I've never done yoga before, does that matter?"

"No, it's fine, I get loads of people coming that haven't done any yoga or meditation before. In fact it's the ideal place to get your practice started, and you will leave feeling that you have a very good understanding of what yoga really is."

Sam booked a room at the next available retreat.

Chapter Three

Grant

Finding Then Living the Dream

"Choose a job you love,
and you will never have to work a day in your life."
Confucius

Grant was on the train again commuting to his job in the city, and looking around at everyone sitting (and standing) in silence. No one looked happy and he wondered if a single one of them actually enjoyed what they spent the majority of their lives doing. He had left school at 16 and gone straight to work in a large department store in central London to earn money to go out and have fun. He saw no reason to stay on at school and have no money when he could be out there living! He had a mortgage by the time he was 21 and was working his way up the corporate ladder. Experience was much more important than useless qualifications in his opinion.

Grant drove the most expensive car he could afford (on HP), and loved his designer suits. Luckily he got a yearly allowance in the menswear department for his uniform, and was not afraid to upgrade to the very best quality and pay the extra from his wages. He knew he looked good, and enjoyed the odd cheeky glance in the mirror whenever he thought he could get away with it. What was reflected back was brown hair parted in the middle and falling on each side to just above his ears. A strong jaw and chestnut brown eyes filled his face, which sat atop a medium frame. He liked being taller than average and enjoyed a boyish charm which went down well with the ladies.

Although he knew deep down that what's on the inside is more important, his appearance still mattered to him greatly. He did sometimes think he was being fickle, but it was hard to go against how society expected you to look, sound and act. He had always tried to keep up with the latest fashions, and even owned some make-up, but no one knew about that and he kept it hidden away safely in his bachelor pad, away from nosey eyes.

Grant was single and had no shortage of female attention and potential partners. He didn't want to be in a relationship, however, as he was young, hot blooded, and having too much fun after all. His flat was flash, bold, and filled with expensive furniture and electrical equipment that he'd purchased at work with his healthy discount. Unfortunately most of it was on his store card, which although had a low %APR, he was at present unable to pay off.

Underneath the cool and trendy exterior was a kind and thoughtful individual whom Grant very rarely let show. He thought he was being weak when he revealed that side of himself.

Grant was happy enough in his job and gave everyday his best, unless it had been a particularly heavy session the night before. His progress from cashier and sales assistant to floor manager couldn't come quickly enough for Grant, and he now had the responsibility of making sure his department ran smoothly and all customers were served swiftly. He had a certain air about him and you could always spot him as soon as you walked into his department.

He was so aloof that some staff were quite intimidated by him. Grant secretly enjoyed the power he sometimes felt when managing up to 50 staff and a few hundred customers. He walked around his department with his head held high, and back straight. Because he was pretty tall he looked downwards to most people, giving Grant an authoritative edge he relished.

Exhausting work

Up at 6am, on the train at 7am, shelf filling for a few extra pennies at 8am before the shop opened at 9am. Then on your feet all day with just a few breaks and of course the obligatory visit to the 5th floor smoking room whenever possible – it was a long day.

Grant got off the tube at Oxford Circus and proceeded towards the escalator along with a few hundred other people all on their way to work. He was excited about today because he was stating a karate course after work and was really looking forward to it.

The day went relatively quickly. There had been a big argument between a couple today, which had entertained the staff for a while, and about 6 security guards had run through chasing after a young bloke in a tracksuit. All in a day's work when you work on the ground floor of a London department store.

Grant got the tills cashed up super quick and was out in record time. He went into the office and got changed then made his way up to the sixth floor meeting room where the class was being held. Sensei Mark greeted him at the door with a little bow and the class started. There were about 14 in the group, most of whom he already knew, and they got started with some kicks and punches.

Starting to ask questions

For some time now Grant had been looking for something. He didn't know what it was, he just knew there was something he needed to do with his life. He enjoyed his job but didn't want to do it forever. Standing on your feet all day and working such long hours was not what he wanted for the future. He didn't feel fulfilled on any level at the end of each day and it all seemed pretty pointless.

The managers in his department had just organised who was going to work over Christmas and New Year (even though it was months away) as the shop was open all through the festive period and everyone wanted time off to celebrate with their friends and families. This year he was unlucky and had to work on New Year's Eve and New Year's Day (first day of the sale), but thankfully had Christmas Day and Boxing Day off.

Grant longed for a job with more sociable hours and which was less demanding physically.

He seemed to pick up the karate sequence quickly and enjoyed the class, but it wasn't quite what he had expected (although he didn't know what he was expecting). He walked back to the tube and waited for his train. The journey only took about 45 minutes this time of night, so much more pleasant than travelling in rush hour when the journey could easily take double that.

As Grant walked through the flat door his cat brushed past him and meowed in hunger.

"Hiya, Arthur."

"Purr purr purr" was Arthur's answer.

"You hungry?"

"Meow."

He fed the cat and himself, turned on the TV and settled into the sofa with his laptop. He started searching the internet for the answer to his question:

What do I want to do with my life?

The weeks went past and Christmas drew ever closer. The shop got busier and the staff became more and more exhausted. It was dark when Grant got to work and dark when he left, but as least he worked on the ground floor and saw daylight – he had friends who worked in the basement or sub-basement who didn't see daylight all week until their day off!

One Tuesday lunchtime Grant was having a cigarette in the smoking room and chatting to his friend Gemma.

"You should try a yoga class," she was saying.

"But I'm not very bendy" he replied.

Gemma laughed. "It doesn't matter if you're not bendy! You'll get more bendy the more you practice."

"But I thought yoga was just for girls."

Gemma laughed even louder. "Oh, you are funny, Grant," she said, "Of course it's for boys too!"

"Well I think I might feel really silly in a leotard with my leg behind my head!" he laughed as well.

"What are you talking about, you'll look great in a leotard!!" Gemma now couldn't stop laughing and was holding her stomach.

"Have you got a spare cigarette I can have as I'm completely out?" Gemma asked once the laughter had subsided.

"Yeah, here you go," Grant passed his pack over. "I guess I

could try out one class to see if I like it and before I go and invest in that leotard!" he said.

"Well, why don't you come with me, then you won't feel so out of your comfort zone. How does that sound?" she offered.

"Sounds great, Gem. What day is it on?"

"Tuesdays, so why don't you come next week?"

"Perfect" said Grant.

> *"Yoga is not about touching your toes,*
> *it's about what you learn on the way down."*
> Judith Lasater

First ever yoga class

That night Grant sat on his computer and did some research into yoga. As it turned out it was mainly men that did yoga in India, where it originated, and all the major types of yoga were created by men. This made him feel a little bit more comfortable about trying it out, and to his relief there were three other men in the class the following week when he arrived with Gemma.

The teacher was very sweet and made him feel instantly relaxed, and they started the session off with some breathing exercises. Grant didn't really understand the diaphragmatic breath and his belly seemed to go in the opposite direction to what it was supposed to! Then they started the stretches and he couldn't believe how stiff his muscles were compared to everyone else's. But it all felt great and he found himself really enjoying the class even though he couldn't do much of it. The worst part of his body, it seemed, was the backs of his legs – wow, they hurt so much. He couldn't touch his toes, in fact he couldn't even get halfway down to his toes!

Chapter Three

Then at the end of the class they did a half handstand against the wall and this he could do. He'd always loved to be upside down as a kid, it felt really natural to him. By the end of the 90-minute session Grant was truly converted and signed up to do the rest of the course. As he chatted to the teacher he even realised that this was something that he would like to teach himself, and he asked the teacher if she thought this might be possible in the future considering his incredibly tight hamstrings.

"Of course," she had said. "You can do anything in life that you put your mind to, and if you work really hard then there is no reason why you can't get really flexible, or be a great yoga teacher."

Gemma and Grant walked to the station together and Grant thanked Gemma for making him go to the class.

"That was great, Gem," he said.

"I just knew you were going to like it," she replied.

"I feel so good now, like, really calm and happy," he said.

"I know, that's how you feel after every class," Gemma said.

"Wow, that's awesome."

They said goodbye as each travelled in a different direction once they got to the station, and Grant sat on his train with a big grin on his face. He felt great.

It was a direction that had never crossed his mind before but it made him feel better than he could ever remember feeling.

As the stations flashed past Grant's mind moved to imagining teaching a yoga class...

There he was at the front of the class and lots of students, mainly women! Some really bendy, good looking women! Tonight's class had been predominantly women. He was going to become even more of a babe catcher ... the idea was growing on him minute by minute.

Finding discipline

It was a real struggle to get up even earlier than 6am to practice yoga first thing and Grant wasn't a morning person at the best of times, so he made a pact with himself that he would do 45 minutes of practice in the evening when he got home. This fitted in much better with his routine and he found himself sticking to it and going over what he had learnt each week in class. His teacher had told him that all he needed to do was remember what she taught that week and keep doing those exercises until the next class. Grant found himself wishing the week away until the next yoga session. He had never felt so passionate about something before – it was like yoga was consuming him.

A month later Grant had got into the swing of practising yoga at home whenever he had an evening in, then would search the internet over his dinner. He researched about teachers that he'd like to study with and courses he'd like to go on. This was actually something that he could do as a living, and he started to make a plan. First he needed to go on some sort of yoga holiday where he could fully immerse himself day and night into yoga, so this was what he started saving for.

Grant's first yoga holiday was for a weekend in Norfolk. The timetable was packed with yoga and meditation and Grant knew this was going to help him decide whether yoga really was the path he was going to pursue on his return to London. His body was becoming bendier and everything seemed to be so much easier than when he started. He cast his mind back to that first yoga class a few months ago and felt a real sense of achievement – he had come so far. He still couldn't touch his toes, but he was definitely getting closer.

He enjoyed turning his phone off for the weekend while

in Norfolk and simply living, eating and breathing yoga. He loved it. He felt so peaceful, content and happy with himself and wished this feeling would last forever.

New perspective

He took a good long look at his life while he was away. It seemed easier to do this when in Norfolk, like the physical distance was being mirrored in his mind.

He looked at his flat, his job, he visualised all the expensive suits in his wardrobe, and for the first time ever it all seemed really pointless. What was he really achieving when he spent too much money? How long did his new possessions bring him happiness?

He was experiencing something completely different right now – feelings of wanting to stop being so materialistic and self-centred and of wanting to help others in some way.

The weekend was an astounding success, he had let the softer part of himself be seen, realising that rather than weakness it was in fact kindness. He had discovered so much about himself in 48 hours and resolved to get to know this kind side better.

Grant knew that this was a long road ahead, and he had to keep his feet on the ground and not get too carried away with all these new insights. The path was very clear to him, but it was not going to be easy to juggle the pull of his old life with the promise of a very different future.

The thought of going back to work, and travelling on the tube felt like torture right now and Grant had to remind himself this was a means to an end. However, he had to admit he was quite looking forward to meeting his mates in the pub later for a few beverages.

Grant's mind was made up after Norfolk and research

began on a teacher's training course. Because yoga originated in India, it seemed the obvious choice, so Grant started to plan a trip to India. He was going to try and get special permission to take an extended holiday from work and even told management he would take some of the time unpaid as he reasoned he needed six weeks away from work. He decided on the course he wanted to take which was for one month in southern India.

The festive season passed and winter had properly kicked in, it was freezing, but the thought of the Indian sun kept Grant going and then he got word through that management had accepted his request for six weeks leave in April/May!

How exciting! Now his plans stepped up a notch and he booked his flight, and place on the course. It was going to be hot in Kerala in April and May as it was pre-monsoon, and Grant loved the heat.

India, my new second home

He landed at Mumbai airport and got a connecting flight down to Trivandrum. The yoga ashram had given very precise instructions as to getting a taxi so that you paid a reasonable price, and ensuring you didn't get ripped off.

Trivandrum is right down on the southern tip of India and as the taxi drove through the town and then up into the mountains, wonderful sights and smells made their way inside the taxi. When they arrived at the ashram it was busy with all the students checking in and finding their way around the grounds. Grant had opted for a private room rather than the dorm as it was only marginally more expensive and he was used to living on his own, plus he didn't much fancy sharing a room with 50 hippy types.

He unpacked and stacked his stuff on the shelves in his

room (no wardrobe) and put a nicotine chewing gum in his mouth. There was no smoking allowed in the ashram he had found out on their website, so he had packed 12 blister packs of the chewing gum. He didn't plan on going back to smoking when he left, but we'll see.

They were not allowed to leave the grounds for the duration of the month's course, and there were guards on the door!

Ashram life

Grant settled into the routine of ashram life easily. Every day was timetabled with very little time outside of classes. A bell sounded in the morning at 5.20am which signalled it was time to get up for morning meditation. It was still dark but when you opened your eyes at the end of the hour's meditation it was getting light and it never ceased to amaze Grant every morning. It was then time for asana (physical postures) practice for 90 minutes which was difficult for the first few days in the heat until everyone acclimatised. Then it was breakfast time and everyone sat on the floor in long rows in the dinner hall as the designated servers each gave you something different. Thali plates were used which are steel plates with different sections, and for every meal there were 3 or 4 different curry dishes, all vegetarian. Additionally there were always either poppadoms or bread and Grant loved the food, and always got seconds or thirds!

During the day there were different classes including the history and philosophy of yoga, chanting, and anatomy. They were all very interesting apart from the chanting class which Grant just couldn't get his head around. He would sit at the back and refuse to take part. It didn't seem right to him to be singing devotional Hindu songs so he chose to sit out seeing as they were not allowed to miss any classes. He had been brought up an atheist and had no strong religious beliefs, and it seemed that Hinduism didn't press any buttons for him. Other Westerners seemed to take Hinduism on fully, wearing only Indian style clothes. He often found these hippy-types tambourine in hand, singing their Hindu hearts out, out by the temple.

Sessions lasted all day and Grant didn't get to bed until at least 10pm every night and that bloody alarm bell went off so early in the morning.

He settled into the routine and after a few days everyone got called into the main hall to find out what their 'karma yoga' was going to be (chores to you and me). Grant prayed for any job other than cleaning the toilets! Anything but the toilets! Thankfully he got clearing up after lunch, which actually was very apt seeing as he loved the food so much. So much so, in fact, that he started to befriend all the people who were on food serving duty – especially the poppadom girl (they often ran out before everyone got a second helping, and she just happened to be really fit too).

There was a really diverse group of people in the ashram and about a quarter of the group were Indian guys, and the rest made up of Brits, Americans, Aussies, loads of South Americans, and the rest Europeans. The youngest was around 18 and the oldest Grant guessed to be in their late 60's. Everyone seemed to be pretty good at their practice, although he'd seen a few people fall out of headstand quite precariously, and everyone was sweating so much.

There was to be no fornicating with fellow students which Grant thought was slightly unfair, as there were some stunning girls, a few of whom had already given him the look. In the second week a couple had been found together on the roof of the women's dorm, and were now banned from even speaking to each other.

Someone stinks

Grant had started to smell curry all the time and couldn't work out where the smell was coming from, when he suddenly realised it was seeping out of every pore of his skin! No one was wearing deodorant and everyone had to wear t-shirts to cover up their shoulders (an Indian custom) so he just went with the flow.

As April progressed the pre-monsoon heat built, but everyone was now acclimatised and Grant found that his body really did stretch further in the warm climate.

Grant had a massive breakthrough one day when doing a forward bend. He touched his toes for the first time ever! It was such a milestone and he had a sudden pang of homesickness when he thought about how he would normally celebrate something important, but quickly realised the boys down the pub wouldn't understand how important touching your toes for the first time would be!

Meditation was getting easier too, it was like his mind had finally realised what was being asked of it, and he could at last switch off. After a meditation session he felt really rested, calm and content, it was the most wonderful feeling. The teachers had told them that because of all the meditation and yoga they were doing, the body didn't need as much sleep as it's normally used to because there is no stress in the body, and Grant could really relate to this as he was only getting about six hours' sleep and feeling unbelievably rested.

I hate exams

As the month long course drew to an end, Grant was getting prepared for the final exams. There was so much information to retain: the different muscles and bones in the body;

rotation; abduction; the asana sequences; the philosophy; The Bhagavad Gita etc…

Grant was doing all his study at night because the day was filled with classes and chores, and suddenly life got all stressful again and Grant had a massive dread of going back home to his job. He couldn't face commuting again and fighting his way in in the morning to a job he didn't really want to do any longer. It all seemed really pointless. Why did he get up so early, get on a packed train, stand up for at least nine hours a day, come home on a packed train, eat, crash, then do the same thing all over again – and he didn't even earn that much.

Panic started to set in as he thought of his life at home and he had to give himself a real talking to to get himself out of this negative way of thinking.

He took himself down to the main hall which was in complete silence and darkness and just sat there with the huge paintings of the Hindu gods all around him. Shiva, Ganesh, Krishna, Durga and Lakshmi among others smiled down on him, and although he didn't feel a huge connection to Hinduism they made him feel calm and safe again that night. He sat there for most of the night hatching a plan. He loved yoga and wanted to make the one thing he felt truly passionate about the central part of his life. What he'd learnt in India was that yoga is a lifestyle, with the physical exercise just a small part of the whole picture. He now wanted to integrate it fully into his life, which meant there had to be some changes.

He knew now that he definitely wanted to teach yoga. What yoga had shown him – that anything is possible – he wanted to share with others. Yoga not only made you feel amazing physically, but also taught you to slow down in life and start to take notice of *everything*. For example Grant thought he had been happy in his job, when in fact he got very little meaningful pleasure from it. He closed his eyes and started to imagine how fulfilled he was going to feel when he started to teach the very thing that made him feel healthy, content and happy. Grant had never felt so sure about anything in his life, and began to feel really excited about the future. He took himself back to his room, had a shower, and crammed in some anatomy revision for an hour before the morning bell sounded.

The exams lasted two days and went better than Grant expected (considering he had hated school and done terribly in his GCSE's). It would appear that he had retained more information than he had realised. He passed with flying colours and it was suddenly time to leave the ashram for the first time in a month.

Being at the beach in India is not like being at the beach in Spain!

A group of nine of them decided to go to the beach resort of Kovalam for a few days (which was pretty close to the ashram) before heading off in their own directions. Grant only had three days before his flight home and welcomed the idea of hitting the beach.

There were only two men in their group of nine and the girls were very pleased to have the boys around as they were getting really pestered by the Indian men.

As it was so hot the girls were wearing bikinis on the beach and in the sea, which was causing a real commotion with the locals. Indian women don't ever take their outer garments off in public and even swim in their sarees.

On the first day they had secured sunloungers on the beach and were all sunbathing in a row. Within 15 minutes there was a crowd of around 30 Indian men at the foot of the beds watching them. The men didn't say anything or make any advances, just looked at them silently. Most of the girls ended up covering up as it was so unnerving and some of them had to leave the beach completely as they felt so uncomfortable. Grant found the whole situation really interesting, and was amazed how the men had no malice towards the girls, they were simply fascinated with them.

The watchers and the watched were equally fascinated by each other in their own ways, and it really was the oddest day at the beach that Grant had ever experienced.

Needless to say they didn't return the following day, instead they hung out in a cool restaurant drinking coffee and eating western food for the first time in a month. Grant had never been much into coffee, always a tea drinker, and since arriving in India had fallen in love with masala chai – a good cup of English tea with added herbs and spices – delicious! It was a drink that he would continue to drink his whole life.

That night they went to a fancy western style restaurant and drank alcohol for the first time in over four weeks. Of course they were all quickly tipsy after the month of clean living in the ashram and ended up on the beach and swimming into the wee small hours.

Grant stumbled up the stairs to his house on stilts above huge rocks at the end of the bay and settled into his last night in India. Tomorrow evening he was flying back to the UK.

His last day was spent buying presents for his family and friends, and a supply of masala chai for himself. He also bought a beautiful blue batik of Ganesh which would sit proudly on his wall at home for years to come.

Grant said goodbye to his new friends and took a taxi to Trivandrum airport. His connecting flight arrived on time in Mumbai and he was soon boarding an Air India flight to London's Heathrow. He loved sitting by the window and as the plane took off he felt a deep pull. He was sad to leave

India, she was like a new friend whose company he didn't want to depart from. But he knew that he would be visiting his friend regularly, and hoped he would see her again soon.

A new way of living

Grant felt different. He now had an important purpose in life - to continue to grow spiritually himself, and to help other people also find internal happiness. He knew that yoga helped to unlock your hidden potential and that everyone was brilliant at something – it was really just a case of taking the time and energy to find out what it was. The very first yoga class that he took had triggered a spark of something within him, and he had followed that spark to India and back, where he had given himself some time to slow down and work out what was important to him.

The very first item on his post India to do list was rewrite his CV to take to local gyms and yoga studios. He wanted to get his first paid yoga job. There were around eight locations that he took his CV to, and while he waited he set up a weekly class for friends and family, to get some practice and experience of teaching. After a couple of weeks of not hearing anything, he made some phone calls to the places that he'd left his CV to make sure it had reached the right people. They had but unfortunately there were no current vacancies at any of the clubs.

He had to be patient.

The next to do item was to cut his hours down at work, to free up some time to set up yoga classes. He had a mortgage to pay, so couldn't leave completely, but needed to start breaking away from his old life. Luckily, because he worked for such a large company, with around 2,500 employees in his branch, this was an easy enough request. He could job share with someone else, it just meant he'd have to move to another department. This didn't bother him as he'd be leaving altogether once his new business had legs.

Grant found a local hall that was inexpensive to rent and decided to set up one daytime and one evening yoga class and charge a minimal fee. It was slow going but he soon had a few regulars who enjoyed his teaching style. He was busy marketing the classes and designing leaflets and had pretty much forgotten about the gyms when he got a phone call from Elite Fitness in Hertford.

First paid yoga class

"Can I speak to Grant, please?" said the person on the other end.

"This is Grant speaking," he said.

"Oh good, this is Mandy from Elite Fitness and I have your CV here," Mandy continued. "Our yoga instructor is unwell and I'm looking for someone to cover the class, could you come in tonight at 7–8pm?"

Grant was jumping up and down, shouting, and waving his hands in the air *in his head*, but calmly said, "Yes, I think I can do that, I'll just have a look in my diary." He rustled the newspaper that was in his lap, took a sip of the masala chai next to him, then coolly came back on the phone, "Yes, I can cover your class, Mandy."

"Oh, thank you so much, Grant. I will look forward to meeting you later."

Mandy put the phone down, and then Grant jumped up off the sofa and did a dance around the room. It was a defining moment, his first ever (fully paid) yoga job.

The class ran smoothly and Mandy's customers were so happy, that he was called back to cover again whenever the need arose. A few months after his first class at the gym Mandy asked if he would like his own permanent class on a Thursday evening.

Grant's class at the gym was a huge success and he built up a steady group who never missed a session. Mandy became a firm friend and he started socialising with the staff and other instructors. It was all going really well and he loved what he was doing.

One day Mandy asked him if he wanted to go for a coffee to talk about an idea she had. They met at a cute restaurant called The Snug and ordered coffee and cake.

Yes please Mandy

He looked across at her. She was a stunning girl, a real natural beauty. She was exactly his type but unfortunately had a boyfriend otherwise he would definitely have had a crack at her.

"Grant, what I'm thinking is that I'd like you to teach more classes at my gym, but rather than just come in as an instructor, how do you feel about us going into business together and setting up a separate business for just yoga and pilates?" Mandy was on a roll and saw that Grant was pretty much speechless. She continued, "I'll teach the pilates classes and you teach the yoga and meditation."

Grant was speechless and his heart was beating really fast with excitement (or was that from too much caffeine) and he had to remind himself to breath deeply before he spoke. "Yes, that sounds amazing," was all he could manage.

Mandy took the lead "We can set up a separate membership that people can take out if they just want to do yoga and pilates, and split the profits 50/50."

Grant left the meeting grinning like a Cheshire cat and as

he sat in the pub with the boys and his pint that night, he reflected on how his yoga business had developed. He was now ready to leave his day job completely and concentrate solely on teaching yoga. He had been back from India only a year and he considered his progress commendable.

Mandy and Grant designed flyers and posters and put a big ad in the local newspaper. On the day of the launch of their new membership they signed up 28 people with many more joining in the coming weeks and months. Grant taught more classes than Mandy, but she was supplying the venue and paying the bills. It was a great partnership.

Reflection

They continued working successfully together and building up their new venture. Grant was really happy about the way things were and that he was now teaching yoga pretty much full time. He also helped Mandy out by sitting on the reception desk in the gym, which he not only enjoyed but was also learning so much about having your own business. Mandy was a very inspiring and highly motivated individual with a successful business and he enjoyed her company.

It was Friday morning and Grant woke up from a long deep sleep. Thursday was a busy teaching day with his first class at 10am, last one finishing at 9.30pm, and classes all the way through in between. He liked to pack everything in like this, then have the following day to take it easy and enjoy the effects of the previous day's teachings and spend the day focusing on his own practice. Yoga cleanses the body and mind, balances and harmonises you physically, mentally and emotionally. All of this from doing just one class, so imagine how he felt after teaching 7 hours of classes the day before! He'd crashed out straight after his dinner and slept so deeply that he'd woken up in the exact same position he'd fallen asleep in. Now he felt high, and it was an all-natural high. His mind was clear, like someone had reached in and pulled all the cotton wool away, and he had an amazing own practice in the comfort of his own flat overlooking the river. How he had progressed! He thought back to that very first class he'd taken with Gemma and how he had struggled to reach even halfway down to his toes. Now he made it all the way with ease. It was truly amazing how his body had changed and opened with practice. He lay down in Savasana (the Corpse pose) and allowed his body to relax and release into the floor. He had been working on twists in his own practice and with his students all week and enjoyed how they quite literally squeezed toxins and tensions out of your body. It was like he was melting into the floor and all his problems followed downwards.

It was not only Grant's inner world that had changed, but also his outer world. He had given his expensive suits and some of his flashy possessions to charity, and was much happier living a simpler existence.

Grant kept in touch with Gemma. They would always have the special connection of yoga and were like kindred spirits.

He looked back on how empty his life had been and felt he owed a lot to his friend Gemma.

Going deeper

Grant understood that, although he was established as a teacher in his own right, there was always the potential to learn more, and he had a yearning to deepen his practice further. He couldn't take a lot of time off as he was so busy, so he started to think about maybe going away for just a few days.

He thought back to the weekend retreat in Norfolk that he had done a few years ago, and looked up the teacher on the internet. Luckily she was still running the weekends with the next one happening the following month. He booked it there and then, and put the date in his diary and in his phone. Excellent.

Chapter Four

Joss

Listening to What Your Heart Says

"Remember that sometimes not getting what you want is a wonderful stroke of luck."
HH Dalai Lama

Joss's relationship had come to an end, their shared property sold, and she had a rather tidy sum of money burning a hole in her bank account and an even bigger burning desire to spend it, and why not? You only live once.

Some people understood why she did it, but most thought she was running away from her responsibilities and from the real world. Joss dismissed it all because she knew exactly where she was going…

She had holidayed on Koh Samui, Koh Pha-ngan and Koh Tao in previous years and always loved 'Amazing Thailand'. Koh Samui seemed like the perfect place to spend a few months and little did Joss know at the time that a few months would end up being six years.

She had found an amazing bungalow on the beach, which was very affordable, and the two Thai sisters that ran the place became firm friends. One of the sisters had an English husband who played some very cool tunes and was quite a well known DJ.

Jumping fish

Life was blissfully relaxed and spent all day on the beach pretty much. Joss loved swimming in the sea and lazing on the beach, and over the coming weeks and months her curly brown hair became blonder, and her olive skin darker.

In the late afternoon fishermen would come down to the beach with large hand nets, as the fish would come close to the shore at this time of day. Joss would watch them skilfully throw the net and it open out like a parachute before landing and then sinking into the water. The fishermen, and Joss, could see where the fish were as they often jumped out of the water. One afternoon Joss was swimming when a shoal swam straight into her. The first fish jumped and hit her squarely in the jaw! Joss laughed as the next one landed in her mouth! They were not big fish but she quickly spat it out before it choked her. She laughed even harder as she turned her back on them and they continued to hit her in the back, it was possibly one of the funniest and most bizarre experiences of her life.

Bophut village was a short walk away along the beach and housed some great restaurants with big trays of fresh fish outside. All you had to do was pick which one you wanted to eat and they'd put it on the BBQ, and Joss definitely liked her fish cooked! She loved the spicy Thai food and felt that she had literally arrived in heaven. It had been a difficult journey leaving her old life behind and many of her friends and some family members just didn't understand her decision.

She had left a well-paid job, broke up with her boyfriend,

sold their house, and rehomed the cat all in the space of two months. On the other hand they had all felt like the easiest decisions she had ever made, and she knew all the way through those two long months that she was doing the right thing. She had no doubts.

Joss smiled to herself as she thought about what she had been through and wondered what was in store for her in the future. She knew she had to find herself a house soon as it just wasn't economical to stay in the beach bungalow, which didn't even have a fridge, so she was paying more for everything. She knew she could get herself a house for under 10,000 baht (£200) a month which worked out to be much cheaper than where she was currently. But there was no rush, she was still in the holiday period, she told herself.

The days and weeks went past and the temperature never dropped below 30 degrees, even when it rained. Joss spent the days watching all that went on around her, listening to the cool tunes being played in the background, and reflecting on all the stories unfolding in front of her.

The tourists walked up the beach into the village with their burnt and blistered bodies, and Joss considered how seriously people took the need to return home from their holiday deeply tanned. She had been exactly the same on arrival to Samui and she thought back to when the urgency had subsided and she had started to sit in her now favourite spot in the shade of a palm tree.

Time to watch life

The weather was incredibly interesting with beautiful cloud formations and storms crossing the island of Koh Pha-ngan opposite. Joss would watch as sheets of rain moved in an easterly direction, hiding parts of the island as it dumped its heavy load. It was quick, and suddenly the island would reappear as the storm whirled off towards its next victim, gathering momentum. Joss had never seen anything like it before, and couldn't take her eyes off these storms when they appeared.

Even when the weather was settled, the wide-open sky seemed to lift Joss, and she realised how much she enjoyed being outside. She was always too cold to be outdoors for long in the UK, and there was little opportunity to look at the sky in the concrete confines of London.

She never seemed to get bored here, and Joss never really had the chance before to truly watch the hive of activity around her without having to rush off somewhere.

The afternoon was drawing in and as the temperature dropped a couple of degrees, the dogs came onto the beach to play and fight. The stray dog population was a huge problem, and you always saw large litters of puppies at every restaurant and hotel it seemed. As soon as a dog wandered onto another's territory the fights would begin, with the sound of wounded animals sometimes penetrating Joss's ears. It was a sickening sound.

The Thai way of life

One afternoon Joss and her three Thai friends were sitting under a palm tree on the beach and discussing their differing cultures.

Toi was the sister of the owner of the bungalow operation Joss was staying in, Nang was a shop owner from the village, and Pia was half Thai half German. They were all very westernised, working in the tourist industry, and it was interesting learning more about Thai life.

"We have many pride," Toi was saying in her enchanting pigeon English.

"What do you mean?" questioned Joss.

"Thai people hating be wrong!"

"Well, I think everyone hates being wrong."

"No, upsetting when argue, we losing pride."

"I don't know if I understand, Toi, do you mean you lose face?"

"Ah, yes! Losing face, Thai people not liking losing face."

"Yes, Thai people not liking admit not knowing. Making them feeling stupid," Nang joined the conversation. "Sometime get Thai people to trouble!"

They smiled at each other and Joss thought how stunningly beautiful these women were.

On cue, Toi's sister Noi came out of the kitchen with a bowl of something she'd just cooked.

"Fry insect," Noi offered the bowl to Joss first. "Is very delicious cooking in chilli and garlic."

"Euww, yuk! That's disgusting!" Joss recoiled in distaste.

"If Thai people offer food, Joss must eating it," Nang told her.

"What, even if I don't want it?!"

"Rude, Joss, if not eating, can upset Thai people."

"But I'm a vegetarian, I don't eat any animals, even insects!"

"Oh…" All four Thai women tucked into the fried delights as Joss looked on and explained herself, as the Thais didn't seem to comprehend the idea of vegetarianism.

Joss had learnt a lot though, and would carry the knowledge of accepting Thai gifts graciously in the future, so as not to upset her native friends.

Their conversation became quite philosophical.

"Are you happy?" Pia asked generally to everyone.

"I thinking so, but wishing have bigger house!" replied Toi.

"You, Joss?" asked Nang.

Joss turned her green eyes from the sunscreen to her friends,

"Blissfully happy, girls. You have absolutely no idea how unhappy I was with my monotonous life back in England," she continued, "it's so dull and cold back home and no one smiles. You're so lucky living here in the 'land of smiles.' "

"Yes, Thailand very beautiful country," replied Toi.

"You stay in Thailand, Joss?" enquired Nang.

"For now, for sure," replied Joss.

"And in future?" asked Toi.

"Well, we'll have to see what happens..." Joss trailed off in thought, then continued, "I'm really happy right now, I'm having such an adventure!"

"If you could have anything, Joss, what would it be?"

"Wow, Pia, there's a very big question!"

Joss lay back and looked up at the sky and watched the clouds roll past. She had never really thought about what exactly she was going to do with her new life. She had created a blank canvas and it was now time to start filling it with all that she dreamt of.

But what did she really want if there were no limits? What was her dream? She started to think outside the box and allow her mind to travel wherever it wanted to go without limitation.

"I would really like to have my own shop, and sell gorgeous clothes and jewellery, and I love being in Thailand with no desire to go anywhere else."

There she had said it! And a growing excitement started to engulf her until she could hardly breathe with anticipation as to what her three friends thought of this crazy idea! Would they think it was stupid? Was it even possible for a 'farang' (foreigner) to open a shop here in Thailand? Joss knew this was a pivotal moment and held her breath until Toi spoke,

"Wow, Joss! That amazing idea! Oh my God! Toi think very good idea!"

And then Pia piped in, "This is very good idea, Joss. You can sell to farang and make big money!"

Joss let out her breath slowly and started to feel a tingling sensation throughout her whole body. It was like her heart had just grown to the size of a football and was beating out of her chest. Perhaps this was actually possible!

"Can a farang have a shop, though?" she asked the girls.

"Possible sure" replied Nang. "There is man in Na Thon is lawyer for farang. I getting his number."

And so the wheels started turning and Joss felt numb as she walked to the bar and ordered four Singha beers.

Oh my god, is this really going to happen?

Toi, Pia and Nang were brilliant and within the next few days Joss had an appointment with Suthep who explained that in fact it was very easy for a farang to set up a company in Thailand, as long as they could afford it!

All four girls went looking in the village to see if there were any available properties suitable for a shop, and there happened to be three for rent. The first one needed a lot of building work and was really expensive anyway. The second one was too far out of the village and wouldn't have good foot traffic. The third one was perfect with the shop unit downstairs and a huge two bedroom apartment upstairs, and all for the negotiated price (by Pia and Nang) of 10,000 baht per month.

It was perfect and Joss signed a 12-month contract with the owner, Pi Mei, and started painting and renovating immediately.

A trip to Bangkok was planned, with Joss travelling by train with Toi and Pia the following week. Everything was moving so fast and felt so right. Her shop was on the beach road in Bophut village, which is a calm part of the island on the north coast away from the party and club scene. In fact it was the only part of the island without any girlie bars, so attracted a maturer, more family orientated crowd. There was only one other shop in the whole village which sold ornaments and not clothing so Joss was sure that she could make a success of her venture. She was excited about the trip to Bangkok, she'd not been on the Thai railway network before and they had an overnight sleeper berth booked.

A train journey through the night

The journey started with a ferry ride to Surat Thani on the mainland, then a short bus ride to the railway station and a three hour wait until their train. They went to the local 7/11 store and stocked up on munchies for the 12-hour journey, then chose the furthest restaurant on the strip, which was packed with Thais. Joss ordered her favourite meal, Pad Kaprow Kung (prawns, onions, chilli and holy basil) 'phet phet' (spicy!) and rice with a fried egg on top.

Finally the train pulled in to the station and they jumped on and found their seats, which were in the second class fan carriage. What an adventure! The windows were pulled down and as the train started to move, the breeze through the carriage was luscious.

There were a few stops before bedtime and street vendors walked through the carriages with drinks and food to sell before themselves getting off at the next stop. Eventually the attendant came around and started to make everyone's beds up. Crisp white sheets and pillow cases were produced and as Joss climbed into her upper bunk, she thought how cosy it was. Unfortunately the cosy feeling wore off as insomnia kicked in, and people kept walking through the carriage, talking on their phones and children crying. She'd always been a light sleeper and spent the whole night tossing and turning. She decided she'd have to buy some earplugs (and maybe valium) for the return journey.

As the train terminated in Bangkok the girls didn't bother to set an alarm, and as it happened they were all awake well before their destination. They had their beds folded back into the chair position and even though Joss had had no sleep she sat there in fascination as the train rolled into Bangkok. There were shanty towns right on the track and she watched people showering using a bucket and tap, and vendors getting their fruit packed in ice and stacked in the carts they would push through the streets.

"Life," sighed Toi.

And they were all fascinated by life and the morning unfolding around them.

Once in Bangkok they got a cab directly to Siam Square and their hotel, White Lodge. It was clean, basic, cheap and central with the sky train on their doorstep. They showered, changed and immediately set off to their first shopping location, the legendary Weekend Market.

I've died and gone to shopping heaven!

Chatuchat market is situated to the north of Bangkok and is easy to travel to on the sky train. They got off at Mo Chit station and made their way down the stairs towards shopping heaven, which covers 35 acres and houses over 8,000 stalls!

The girls knew exactly where to go and guided Joss through the crowds to a side entrance. Joss would follow this route on all subsequent lone visits to the weekend market and would navigate to her favourite stalls without ending up in the dreaded pet section. Witnessing hundreds of unhappy and unhealthy caged animals was not on her list of things to experience in Bangkok!

It was early but already everyone seemed to be out shopping. They made a beeline for a coffee shop Pia knew of, and had coffee and Phad Thai for breakfast. Perfect.

Joss was looking for naturally made products, primarily clothes and shoes made of cotton, linen and hemp. She was also on the hunt for semi-precious stones to sell as jewellery and as ornaments. The girls scoured up and down the lanes packed with goods and Joss was really pleased with what she found. She had a nice even amount of clothing, jewellery and stones from the market, and what an experience it had been.

After their second day in the market the girls had a rest day and took it easy in the morning then got a cab to China Town and followed the street all the way down. Joss found some more suppliers here and picked up hemp flip-flops and jewellery. The crowds were thick here too with a beggar laying on the floor and wiggling his amputated leg in the air. It was a shocking sight to Joss, but one which was repeated two or three times during the afternoon. Her Thai friends seemed to pay no notice, but it upset Joss.

In the evening they took a cab to the Khao San Road, which is the hub for farang travellers, but there was nothing that Joss wanted to buy there so they got some dinner and went back to their hotel.

Bangkok was hot and crowded and such a complete contrast to life on the islands, but reminded Joss of how much she had missed city life. In the coming few years Joss would repeat this journey many times and built a strong relationship with her Bangkok suppliers, and enjoy her city fix.

Valium time

The next day the girls made their way to the railway station laden with huge bags (thank goodness Joss had some helpers!) and got settled in their train seats. This time they set their alarms as the train was going all the way down to Hat Yai near the Malaysian border, and they had a ferry to catch at 7am at Surat. This time Joss managed a few hours sleep, courtesy of her newly purchased earplugs and half a valium, and thank God she did, as the remainder of the journey was a complete nightmare. They had somehow been taken to the wrong ferry terminal and would have to endure a five hour journey on a much smaller boat rather than the one and a half hour journey that had been booked. The girls were ranting in Thai to the bus driver who had given them the wrong information. The ferry operator was unhappy too because they had too much luggage for his small boat!

In the end it was all sorted but the Thai girls were grumpy because they had to sit in the sun on this farang boat for five hours (Thais hate being in direct sunlight) and Joss didn't tell them quite how much she did enjoy the sunbathing opportunity – *well she was a farang!*

The journey was over eventually and Toi's sister Noi picked them up in her truck once they arrived back on 'the rock', and drove everyone home. Joss unloaded her wares and excitedly dumped them in the shop before retiring upstairs for a nap.

The next decision Joss had to make was a name for her shop. She sat in one of the local bars with Toi and Pia and they tossed names into the mix:

"Joss shop," said Toi.

"Boss Joss," laughed Pia.

"Come on, help me and be serious," Joss asked her friends.

"Life," said Toi.

"Natural Life," toyed Joss.

"Natural World."

"Inner World."

"No, I was thinking about something more earthy, more natural, because all the things I'm selling are natural fabrics," Joss continued, "and the crystals and stones…"

They continued to play with ideas and then suddenly Joss had it: "Inner Guidance," she said. And she loved, loved, loved it!

"It's perfect!" she said "It's got a certain ring to it, and people will feel like they're being guided around the shop once they come in!"

Inner Guidance is born

Inner Guidance opened in the January and was an instant success. The tourists loved what she was selling as it was completely unique to the village. Joss lit candles every night outside the shop and played chilled out music for herself and her customers. Directly next door to her was a hairdresser's which was owned by a lovely Thai lady, Lek, and they shared a marble table and chairs outside their shops where they sometimes ate together. One night Joss sat on Lek's side and looked towards Inner Guidance. A sudden sense of pride and achievement washed over her. She had been so busy in the last few months that she'd not had time to reflect on what she had accomplished. There were not many young western women with their own shops in Samui! Joss knew she was stubborn and strong willed, but what she had not realised up until that point was quite how much trust she had in herself. The shop had, in fact, been ridiculously easy to open because everything had felt right and happened seamlessly. She'd had no doubt that what she was doing was as it was supposed to be, and it had all started with the question *"If you could have anything, what would it be?"*

Joss decided there and then that she would keep asking herself that same question regularly, like checking in with herself, her feelings and the direction she was going in.

Soon the time came for Joss to employ someone to work in the shop. She let her Thai friends know of her request and a lady called Tiew turned up one day to apply for the position. Tiew was middle-aged but very young at heart, and spoke excellent English. She had worked for farang for years and had even had an English boyfriend or two.

Tiew was an artist and Joss thought of all the wonderfully creative jobs she could do around the shop. She was perfect and was given the job on the spot.

The shop's first year was more successful than Joss had dared to imagine and she was now in a position to fly to Bangkok for her shopping trips, which made life super easy. Bangkok Airways ran their first and last flights of the day at a huge discount so it became economical as well as easy to fly with her large amounts of shopping.

Marmite, love or hate it!

There were certain Western foods that were not available on the islands, so Joss had them sent over either by post or with people visiting Samui. One of these must-haves was Marmite. Now you either love it or hate it, and Joss thought it would be very interesting to find out on which side of the fence her Thai friends sat.

They all went into her kitchen one day where Joss popped some bread in the toaster, and unscrewed the Marmite jar. The girls had never come across it before, but Joss wouldn't let them even smell it until the toast was buttered and Marmite spread on.

Tea was made too, and they took it and their plates of Marmite on toast out onto the balcony. Joss steamed into hers. She'd not had a delivery for ages so was in much need of her Marmite fix.

"EUUUW!!!" shrieked Toi.

"HORRIBLE!!!" chorused Pia.

Joss laughed, she had expected that reaction, and it meant more toast and Marmite for her!

"Disgusting food, Joss," remarked Toi. "How can you liking this?"

As the year drew to a close Joss's landlady came over to the shop. She generally kept to herself so Joss knew the visit was significant. Her one year's contract was up for renewal and her landlady informed her the rent was going up from 10,000 to 20,000 baht per month!

"You pay me now for year" Pi Mei told her.

Joss had paid for her first year in advance with the understanding (she thought) that she would be able to pay monthly in the future, and although Inner Guidance was successful she certainly didn't have a spare 240,000 baht (£5,000) hanging around!

Pi Mei gave her one month's notice and disappeared into her house.

Joss felt like her whole world was crashing in. She was doing what she loved to do, so why was this happening? She left the shop in Tiew's capable hands and went to find her friends. She got quite drunk that night and it turned out this had been happening to quite a few other westerners too. Just like Joss, when their contracts were up they were also being slapped with 100%+ rent hikes. She awoke the next morning feeling very sure that she should find herself a new premises and continue doing what she loved so much. So a new search party was sent out in the coming days to find the next venue for Inner Guidance. Rent prices had gone up in the last year and the village had got much busier with more western businesses (Suthep the lawyer for farangs was doing a roaring trade and had had to move to bigger premises himself). Most houses and units were either full or too expensive for Joss. They walked all the way down to the crossroads when Pia suggested they continue walking past the pier to the much quieter end of the village.

"But no one comes down here," Joss stated.

"You putting sign up at pier for your shop," suggested Toi.

"Location, location, location," said Joss "is the most important factor for any retail shop."

"Well, let's take a look" urged Pia.

They passed a bakery on the left with Aquademia scuba diving school opposite, then two Thai restaurants and new luxury apartments right on the beach. Then on the right a FOR RENT sign on a beautiful wooden house. Joss knew immediately that this was Inner Guidance's new home. She definitely had concerns about being slightly off the beaten track, but knew that she could make this original Chinese fishing house far more appealing than the small concrete unit she was leaving. The owners had built a big concrete monstrosity behind the original house and three generations were living like westerners with air conditioning and other mod-cons. Joss fell in love with the idea of living like a Thai, in her 100 year old teak wood house. Their roles had been reversed and everyone was happy!

The new rent was 10,000 baht per month, paid monthly, which Joss couldn't believe she was paying for this beautiful house. The shop would look stunning with the teak backdrop and Joss asked Tiew to organise some shoe racks and clothes rails to be made out of bamboo. How exciting! She was following her heart again and it felt amazing.

The next month was spent getting the new house ready and moving everything across. There was now so much space that Joss even had room for a chill-out corner where they would eventually set up a herbal tea area with a selection of self-help books on some shelves for customers to read whilst chilling and drinking. Some new signs were organised which Tiew painted herself and Pia donated some huge plants to live outside. It looked stunning by day, but really came into it's own at night when the candles were lit. Customers told Tiew and Joss that they simply *had* to stop and have a look inside because the place looked so great. Inner Guidance literally pulled people in!

Life settled back down in their new location, with high season, rainy season and low season passing by.

Wow, what a journey Joss had been on to get to this point! She thought back to her old existence in England and it seemed like looking at a different person's life. It scared her to think about what she would be doing now if she'd not had the courage to believe in her dreams, as she had many friends who were 'stuck' in unhappy jobs and relationships. She knew how lucky she was to have had the opportunities that presented themselves to her, but credit where it was due, she had fought for her freedom and happiness. You only live once (she was living in a Buddhist country though so she couldn't really get away with this saying!) so why not really do your best and enjoy life as much as possible?

Another great aspect of living on Samui was the massage and spa revolution. Thais give the best massages and for just 250 baht (£5) you could be transported into complete heaven for an hour or two. Joss had a few favourite masseuses around the island and had at least one massage per week. One of her favourite locations for a massage was Spa Samui in Lamai. They also had a fabulous restaurant serving vegetarian Thai and western delights. Joss was a regular with her favourite dishes being massaman mash, zut-zut soup, Greek salad and the San Bao special. Delicious!

Spa Samui's main purpose, however, was detox fasting which everyone agreed was the most ironic thing ever. It meant that most people who were staying in the resort were not eating for anything between 3 and 30 days, but the restaurant was voted in the top 50 in the world a few years back!

No food for seven days…

Joss had talked to many people fasting over the years and decided she was going to give it a go. She gave herself a week off and booked into the resort. She didn't want to drive back and forth from Bophut to Lamai everyday as many fasters had told her you can sometimes go a little crazy within the seven days of no food. (No surprise there!)

She had followed the pre-cleanse diet for three days of raw fruit and vegetables, had a pretty good night's sleep in her new surroundings, and was ready at 7am for her first round of supplements. These include psyllium husk and bentonite clay which when mixed with water or juice becomes like wallpaper paste and you have to drink it really quickly before it sets. This solution then moves down through your digestive system and starts a cleansing process. It's like a baby's bottle brush and helps to pull out old food that might be stuck in the wall of your intestines.

…oh, and a tube up your arse

The next activity on the daily timetable was 90 minutes of yoga followed by Joss's first attempt at colonic irrigation. She was definitely not looking forward to sticking a tube up her bum then pumping gallons of warm water and coffee up and then back down!

Because it was her first day, someone had brought the bucket to her room and showed her how to set everything up. She had attended a talk the previous evening with others who were starting the fast that day, where they were talked through the details of self-administered colonics. They were also given their own 'tip', which is about the size of a pen casing and the connection between plastic tube and anus.

Joss took her tip out of its plastic bag and attached it to the tubing that was sticking out of the 'hood' of the colema board. The colema board is around 6 feet long and big enough to lay down on. The end with the hood is placed over the toilet (seat up), with the other end placed on a chair. The board is now horizontal and ready. A bucket is placed on a hook in the ceiling with the coffee and water solution and tubing running down from the bucket and into a hole in the hood. This end of the tubing sits inside the hood which is where the tip is connected.

Joss lay down on the board and placed a pillow under her head. She was very anxious. A small jar of Vaseline was provided and she smeared the tip and herself with it. It was now crunch time and for the first time in her life Joss attempted to insert something into her anus.

It didn't go well. It just wouldn't go up! And there was no point in pushing because it really hurt when she did that. She was getting really stressed now so she gave up for a bit and did some of the breathing they'd done in yoga earlier.

"Relax, Joss," she said out loud "Breathe."

It seemed to help, so she reinserted and tried again. The tip felt like it had moved upwards so Joss unclipped the tube and allowed some water to flow from the bucket and up her bum.

Unfortunately it just squirted all over her buttocks, as the tip had not in fact gone inside her.

"Bollocks" she said and got all stressed again.

"Breathe in, 1-2-3, breathe out, 1-2-3," she repeated over and over in her head with her eyes closed, until she felt calmer.

It crossed her mind to give up, but she couldn't do that because she really wanted to detox her body and mind. She'd seen these fasters before with their bright white eyes and clear skin and she wanted some of that. She'd also seen them in complete meltdown as the toxins leave the body and make you feel rubbish, just before you start to feel amazing.

She'd got off the board to check the time and was dismayed to find that 25 minutes had passed and she'd got absolutely nowhere. The warm water would be cold soon and therefore less effective so she'd better get a move on. She gave herself a proper talking to whilst pacing up and down and practiced some more deep breathing.

"Back on board, girl," she giggled at her own joke and applied more lube.

"Come on, you can do this," she gently encouraged herself and as her mind started to let go of the stress of the whole situation, so did her anus.

The sensation of water entering your rectum and travelling up your descending colon is a strange one and not something Joss could particularly put into words.

"It felt like my left side was going to explode" she later discussed at the dinner table with her fellow fasters. They were 'eating' broth which was the hot water used for cooking vegetables in other dishes, which they could add garlic, cayenne pepper and/or herbs (without eating any of course!) to add more flavour (some said it tasted like dishwater).

"Once I finally got in, it was fine" she continued.

"I hated it," another faster replied

"I had loads of mucoid plaque come out and maybe a worm too!" a faster called Ian shared.

"Well, I have to say that I didn't look at what came out!" Joss retorted.

"Get yourself a basket to put in your toilet bowl next time and check it out" Ian said helpfully.

"Mmmmm, maybe," replied Joss.

"I gave myself a great massage today," said Naomi, a regular faster.

"What while you were doing your colonic?" enquired Joss.

"Yes," Naomi replied. "When the water comes in, try and hold it there for as long as you can and massage your colon," everyone was silent and waiting for more information. Naomi continued "it helps to break away the plaque that lines your intestines, which is made up of old food that your stomach couldn't digest, which is probably what Ian saw in his basket."

There was lots of new information to gather about the body and how to live healthier, and professionals on hand to give you wonderful treatments. Joss tried out yoga, meditation, chi kung, numerology, a floatation tank, acupuncture, body tapping, and a cranial sacral treatment. There was also a fabulous tea ceremony hosted by San Bao where everyone sat around and drank oolong tea, something that Joss would continue drinking over the coming years, due to its numerous health benefits.

Thankfully the second and subsequent colonics were much more successful after the disastrous start, and Joss even took some photos of what came out!

Day one and two consisted of getting out of the routine of eating and into the new routine of supplements, yoga, colonic, massage, lunch (broth), supplements, treatment, colonic, dinner (broth), steam, supplements, and bed.

Toxins come to the surface on days three and four

Days three and four were the killers, and Joss struggled to do anything at all with the banging headache and all over itching. These were classic symptoms of toxins coming up to the surface of the body. It takes the body around 24 hours for the digestive process to stop, and once this function has ceased, the body goes off and starts making repairs to itself now that no energy is needed to digest food. Everyone assured Joss that what she was feeling was normal and she just needed to ride it out, but that was easier said than done when you felt awful, and for two days she struggled through the timetable and spent all free time in her hammock on her balcony.

The morning of day five was like being born again! Joss felt amazing. She got up and looked at herself in the mirror. Her eyes were really white now and skin glowing, yes, she had made it through the past two days without losing her marbles (many had) and her head felt so clear and toxin free that she could think really clearly. She bounced to the supplement counter and then off to yoga, which she'd missed for the last two days.

After yoga, as she sat drinking a fresh coconut, her group of friends were discussing what they were going to eat to break the fast. This was, they'd been told, as important as the fast itself. You can shock your body by not eating the right food if you've not eaten anything for seven days.

Joss was going for papaya as were most others, with a simple salad later. The last few days were the most enjoyable as she had tons of energy, felt amazing and tried to cram in as many treatments as possible. She was going back to work in a few days and wouldn't have time to do any of this stuff once she was back so she well and truly made the most of it.

Most people who enjoy the fasting experience complete one

every couple of years to keep the toxins out, and remain as healthy as possible in between. It can also act as a springboard for anyone wishing to get out of some unhealthy eating patterns. Joss even spoke to someone with a very serious disease who was fasting rather than using conventional medical treatment.

How can a plate of papaya make me cry?

Day seven finally arrived and Joss inserted her probiotic supplement via an anal syringe, to give her intestines some healthy bacteria, and was then ready to eat!

A gorgeous plate of papaya was served and she squeezed a quarter of lime over it. It was delicious, in fact there was so much flavour she felt like her mouth might not cope. The whole experience was quite humbling.

She sat in silence and was glad she was sitting alone as she had a moment of absolute gratitude for all that she had, and she had so much: to have the opportunity to choose not to eat for health reasons, when so many millions of people on the planet were starving; the ability to realise how lucky she was, when so many walked through life blindly; to be in a situation where she had so much choice over job, location, freedom. This had already been the most wonderful experience, but now she was deeply touched by the first taste of food in seven days and would never again take anything for granted, but least of all the food she ate.

Inner Guidance beckons

Joss said goodbye to the staff and her new friends, vowing to continue with the regular yoga, meditation and healthy eating. She left with take-away Greek salad and Vietnamese spring rolls which were more favourite items from the menu. Tiew was very pleased to see her, as was her cat PiSua.

One of the many attractions of living in Thailand was the freedom that one feels. The West is full of laws, restrictions, and health and safety measures. There just didn't seem to be any red tape in Thailand and it left Joss feeling very free. The only time she ever saw the police enforcing motorcyclists to wear a crash helmet was the odd road block outside a police station every now and again, and this was simply to pick up the 200 baht fine (to put straight in their pockets she suspected).

Obviously this lack of law was not safe, and there were many deaths on the roads. This was probably Joss's least favourite aspect of life in Samui, it seemed like you ran the gauntlet every time you were on the roads. But Joss was about to experience how the freedom she so loved was about to turn on her, and a catalogue of road traffic accidents would ultimately send her back to England.

The beginning of the end

The first of four road accidents took place just outside Bophut on the main ring road around the island (also known to the Brits as the M25). Joss was the passenger in her Thai friend's truck as they turned right across traffic into Monkey Theatre Road. Traffic was backed up and someone had stopped to allow them to turn right. They did turn but unfortunately the girl on the motorbike on the inside did not see them and slammed hard into the front passenger side of the truck, right next to Joss.

Everyone got out of the car, and Joss's Thai friend who had been driving quickly told her to go home and get away from the scene immediately. Joss understood and slipped away as everyone else went to see how the girl was.

She may have been wrong but over the years of living in Thailand Joss had witnessed an assumption that all Westerners are rich, and if a Westerner is caught up in any kind of road accident, even if it is not their fault, they have to pay hospital bills, damages, and sometimes compensation. A Westerner was automatically guilty and had to prove their innocence it would seem.

Joss knew she would always be viewed an outsider, and tried to understand and accept the different customs and laws of the foreign land she was living in, but sometimes it felt hard and unjust.

In this instance Joss knew that her friend was protecting her, and as the incident had nothing to do with her, it was much less complicated to leave the accident site for the Thais to sort it our fairly. It turned out that the girl was not too badly hurt, thank goodness.

Accident number two was when Joss was still quite new to riding a motorbike herself, was wearing wholly inappropriate footwear, and got her little toe stuck in the wrong direction when breaking sharply, ouch!

Luckily after several stitches to keep the toe on, and the wearing of a splint to allow the bone to mend, she was as good as new. The lesson she had leant was to not wear flip-flops on the bike!

Attempted murder

Accident number three was also on her motorbike but this time was not her fault. She was driving home after her cousin's wedding at a beautiful resort in the far north of the island, and probably going around 50kmh. she had a long thin dress on, jumper with a zip, closed in shoes and no helmet. It was very late and the roads were empty.

She suddenly sensed that someone on a bike was driving up really close to her, on the inside. Why were they over taking her on the inside?

The next thing she was aware of was a foot coming towards the back wheel of her bike.

As the wheel was taken out and Joss tumbled to the floor, another cyclist drove on the outside of her and took the handbag that was over her right shoulder. She fell awkwardly, but amazingly didn't hit her head.

Shock and confusion engulfed her and she lifted herself off the ground and started searching for her handbag at the side of the road.

This had all happened outside a shop and the owners came out to see what had happened. The Thai man picked up her bike from the middle of the road and parked it in his drive. They led Joss inside the shop and asked her to tell them what happened and was there anyone she wanted to contact? Slowly her foggy head started to clear and she realised she didn't have anyone's phone number because all the numbers were in her phone, which had been stolen, and it took her a minute to pull herself together and think of someone's number. All shops have the Samui guide books in them, and one of her good friends Su's business was listed. She called the number, told Su what had happened and Su told her she was on her way. As Joss put down the phone she burst into tears as the shock started to subside and the reality of the situation took hold.

She looked down and both bloodied knees were sticking out of the beautiful dress she had bought in Bangkok, and she was covered in blood. Luckily all her injuries were below her shoulders and she didn't appear to have any broken bones.

Su and Lucy came to pick her up and they drove straight to the police station where Joss gave a statement. Su then insisted that she come stay with her, as Joss would be very sore the next day. They stopped off to buy antiseptic lotions and potions, gauze and cotton wool.

Joss had to literally peel her dress from her wounds before she could apply the cream. It was not a pretty sight. She crawled into bed and it felt like she slept for a thousand years.

In the morning she was in agony. She couldn't sit up at all which led everyone to diagnose a broken rib or two. Joss refused to go to hospital, instead taking up Su's kind offer of hospitality.

Her recovery was slow but sure, and she had loads of time to think things over. The first thing she decided was to get rid of her bike and get a car, a much safer option, as she didn't want to go through this again.

Drink driving was a massive problem on Samui, and you could be the safest driver in the world, but still get caught up in other people's bad driving. Having any kind of accident when on a bike was dangerous because everyone wore light clothing due to the warm weather. She would hire a jeep from now on.

The second decision Joss made while recovering was that her attackers must have needed what they stole from her more than she did. It was a few months after the devastating Tsunami, and although geographically Koh Samui had not been affected, the island had seen a rise in crime, tourists and homeless Thais in the ensuing months.

Joss believed that it was probably a group from the mainland that had been touched in some way by the horrific events of 26th December 2004 and this belief made it easier for her to forgive them, although everyone else thought it was attempted murder.

The police got in contact with her a few weeks after the mugging asking her to come down for a line-up as they had made an arrest. Joss reiterated that the only thing she saw that night was a shoe coming towards her. She never saw his face, so there was no point.

Eventually she was healed enough to go back to work but she would always bear the scars on her right ankle, knee and hip.

Four out of four – the big one

Joss was a thousand times happier in her jeep! She would play music really loud and sing her heart out as she drove in the sunshine. She was really happy and had no idea that her life was about to change so dramatically.

She knew the island like the back of her hand and this particular morning was driving the backroads on the west coast of the island. Joss approached a quiet t-junction and turned left. The jeep hadn't even come out of its turn when Joss saw a bike come flying around the curve of the road she had just turned into, going too fast to stop in time. She stopped the car completely and it was like the bike came towards her in slow motion. He also knew he was going to hit her and thank God he was wearing a crash helmet as he was about to crash big time.

He hit the jeep head-on and went over the top of the bonnet and then fell underneath the car. Joss got out and saw him conscious but unable to get up. Some Thai people came running from nowhere and started to point and shout at Joss, and tend to the injured man. Joss found herself in shock again and felt like in a trance as she called a Thai friend, explained she needed his help NOW, and sat by the side of the road helpless as an ambulance arrived and took the young Thai man away. The Thai crowd walked away still shouting and obviously still accusing her, although she had done nothing wrong. She looked at the damaged bike, split helmet, blood and tissues on the floor and started to take photos of the scene to prove her innocence. The photos clearly showed her car on the correct side of the road and the bike on the wrong side of the road.

Her friend Moo finally arrived just before the police, who had been alerted to the accident, she guessed, by the hospital or the unfriendly crowd.

She refused to drive the jeep, so Moo drove them to the police station where once again she would have to make a statement. They waited for news from the hospital about the state of the bike driver, which was not great, but he was alive.

Joss showed the police the pictures she had taken at the scene to make it clear that she had done no wrong. She knew the truth had a habit of morphing into something different in these situations if they were allowed to get out of control. She was so pleased she'd thought of taking the pictures, and that she happened to have her camera with her, but she was very, very scared.

Do you have a warm heart?

The policeman then told her that the young man's mother was at the station to see Joss to ask for money, as they couldn't afford the huge hospital bill that was sure to follow. The policeman told Joss that the family sold fried insects at the side of the road and were very poor.

"If you have warm heart, you give money" the policeman told her.

It was agreed that 3,000 baht (£62) would mean Joss had a warm heart, and the family could pay the expected hospital bill.

Moo and Joss left the police station and Moo drove her home. It had been the worst day of her life.

The shock wouldn't go away, and Joss felt like she was going to feel like this forever. She was numb. How could this happen to her? It all seemed so out of her control. It could have been worse, sure, if the guy hadn't been wearing his helmet, but she still had so many emotions flying around her head.

Primarily she had a sense of vulnerability that she'd not experienced before. She was a foreigner living in another's land, and she had never before felt so alone and isolated. It seemed to her that on the whole life was really great in Thailand, but when things went wrong they went really wrong, like what had happened today.

She was questioning everything now. Did she want to stay in a country whose people could turn on her in an instant? She no longer felt safe, it was like walking a highwire, with a bottomless pit underneath. If you fell, you were lucky to survive.

And the injustice of it all.

Joss started to feel homesick which was a new feeling for her. She longed for enforced right and wrong rather than corruption. She found herself longing for the safety found within the West's rules and laws.

It's time to go home

As soon as that thought entered her head, it would not leave. Suddenly everything that had meant something to her no longer held any appeal. Living here suddenly felt like it was all on the surface, without any depth, and once you scratched the surface it was ugly underneath.

Now she longed for England which was ugly on the surface (cold, grey, rainy, grumpy, moany), but underneath held everything that made Joss feel safe, secure and happy. Her family, her friends, her values, and her foundation.

Joss was absolutely certain that she was going home, and was amazed that such a life-changing decision could happen since she woke up that very morning. It was very clear to her that it was time to leave Thailand.

Her business was sold as a going concern to a lovely Russian lady called Anna, and Joss shipped home the items in her shop and home that she didn't want to part with.

PiSua was rehomed and Tiew found herself another English business to work for.

Everything was sorted and her plane ticket purchased. Joss was off to England where she would crash with friends for the time being.

Transition

On the 13-hour flight home Joss reflected on her six years away from the UK. She'd had an amazing experience living in Thailand and didn't regret anything. She was, however, very happy to be returning to where she felt she belonged, and was excited about seeing everyone.

Joss pondered whether or not she had run away from her problems all those years ago, but was just happy that she was able to return and make it right with a few special people whom she had desperately missed. There were many Brits that she'd befriended in Samui that couldn't leave and make it right with their friends and family because they'd left it too long, or left on such bad terms. She was super lucky and felt like she had been given a second chance, and was going to make the most of being back home.

Travelling was great but shouldn't be done to mask what is really going on in your life, or used to run away from problems or brush them under the carpet. Issues have to be dealt with at some point. Joss had learnt that dealing with them sooner was far easier than leaving them to grow and develop into increasing bitterness.

Joss pushed the button so that her seat was as horizontal as possible and closed her eyes. She was still hungry because she couldn't stomach the airline food after her detox, but was tired and decided it was time for a nap. She was nervous and excited about her return, knowing that it was not going to be easy to adjust back to the cold, or the rules, or not having her own place. But she absolutely knew that she was doing the right thing, and was getting used to following her heart. Her heart had led her to Thailand and now back again, and she felt she had grown so much and become more comfortable in her own skin. Six years in Asia had made her stronger, more confident, and what an adventure she had had!

She was bringing so much more to the table now, and although it was only six years, she felt so much wiser than when she had left the UK.

She opened her eyes and glanced out of the window at the landscape below and the thousands of tiny twinkling lights flickering in the darkness.

Joss mentally closed the Thailand chapter and watched as the next page turned. It was titled UK and lay there blank. It was up to her what words would be written and she smiled in the dark cabin and wondered how many of her fellow passengers knew they were writing their own life story with every word, thought, feeling and action they had. Or whether they felt powerless as life seemed to push them along, just like the wind pushes clouds endlessly through the sky.

Joss knew she was lucky to have this knowledge and understanding that life was what you make it. She had taken hold of life's controls and was in the captain's seat. She laughed to herself. She had absolutely no idea what she was going to do, but did not feel too worried about this, she was going to keep following her heart.

Sleep was now coming and Joss' last thought was of taking her first step back on UK soil.

Joss knew she had to have a plan for her transition between Thailand and the UK and, before leaving Thailand had booked onto a yoga and meditation retreat. She'd enjoyed the yoga she'd done in Thailand and hoped this would smooth the way for the changes ahead, particularly as the teacher leading the weekend had herself spent time teaching at The Spa in Lamai. Joss was believing less and less in coincidence so took the cue, and was keen to meet Jo.

Joss sat back and fell asleep with a smile on her lips.

Chapter Five

Meg

Creating a Space for Yourself Away From the Madness

"Sometimes it takes losing everything you have to finally grow and find yourself."
Unknown

Meg was seriously struggling.

She had been for a while now but was in complete denial. It's a hard thing to admit that your business is failing and you hardly have enough money to feed yourself.

But it was now very clear that something had to give and by chance it was a visit to see her accountant that led to one decision that was to turn her life upside down. She thought back a couple of years to where it had all started...

Meg had moved to a new area three years earlier after the breakdown of her relationship and had quite literally reinvented herself. No one knew her history or her story, her life was a blank canvas on which she could paint any scene.

After the break-up Meg had turned to food for company and gained around 25 pounds. She was just shy of 5 foot 2 inches and had become quite rotund. With her short mousy bob and sharp fringe, she hid well her chubby face.

Meg liked to read and had a huge collection of self-help books where she had read many interesting things that had helped her through some pretty tough times. She had read about vision boards which are made from a large piece of paper, preferably A3, on which you place pictures of what you dream about. You are visualising your goals and imagining that your dream job, relationship, home and health, etc. are already real. The pictures help you to get to that place in your head that you actually believe this can happen. Meg created her own one with the emphasis on good health and a new career.

On her vision board she had a picture of herself in her weight prime and was determined to achieve that once more, along with a healthy happy relationship and successful business (not much then!).

Buying a franchise

She wanted to work for herself and soon an opportunity had presented itself to her to buy into a children's yoga franchise. The company promised Meg that there was great demand for yoga in schools and that schools were prepared to pay a high price for the service. Meg would employ teachers to deliver the classes whilst she drummed up business and grew her team. The franchise was expensive to purchase but sold in an extremely convincing way. Meg signed up and soon had four teachers trained up and teaching classes for her. The bank loan was huge but the projected figures that the franchisor had guaranteed showed a quick return on her investment, and big profits into the second year, which not only excited Meg but her sorry looking bank account too.

Meg loved the work but schools didn't seem to have

the money to spend on her classes. She was not reaching her targets, but neither were other franchisees that she'd befriended. It would appear that the franchisor had beefed up not only the demand for children's yoga but also the finances.

The slip downwards into serious financial difficulties was slow, and it was a little over a year later that Meg found herself taking cash out on one of her credit cards to pay the minimum payments on her other credit cards. She knew at that point that she was spiralling out of control. She took advice from the franchisor who told her to contact her bank and ask for a further £8,000 on her existing £2,500 business overdraft. (£10,500 in total!)

Stupidly she did ask the bank and thankfully the bank said "*No way*".

She was left not knowing which way to turn as her business was not generating enough money to pay everyone. Her first priority was to pay her teachers, then her bills/loans/overdrafts, and that was where the money ran out. There simply was not enough money to pay the franchisor's monthly percentage or herself. Meg was struggling to do a proper weekly food shop and found herself living off fish finger sandwiches, which was doing nothing for her rapidly expanding waistline.

Bankruptcy

The end of the financial year was fast approaching, and Meg had been putting off making an appointment with her accountant. Not only was she dreading facing the actual losses that her company had acquired, but she didn't even know how she was going to pay her accountant. She knew it was a mess but it was much easier to pretend it wasn't happening.

As the deadline got closer Meg had absolutely no choice

but to pluck up the courage to make the appointment, which was scheduled for later in the week. Meg took along all her paperwork (she was very good at keeping everything organised) and with a heavy heart sat opposite her accountant Neil.

"Meg, it's good to see you," he said.

"Yes, good to see you too, Neil, but I'm afraid things have got much worse since the last time we spoke." Meg was surprised how good it actually felt to be honest about her finances, rather than the customary, "Yes, everything is great," nonsense that she would say to people in passing, if they asked.

"I had feared that would be the case, Meg and I'm really sorry to hear confirmation of what I suspected," Neil continued "Let's have a look at your profit and loss spreadsheet and why don't you run through what's going on."

The two of them sat for around half an hour breaking down all the figures when Neil suddenly said something that stunned Meg.

"I think you should go bankrupt, Meg."

The words hung in the air for what seemed like ten minutes before Meg finally replied, "You are joking."

"No, Meg. You have got over £30,000 of debt through this business with no way of paying it back, and you have no assets. It is my advice that this is by far the best course of action for you."

They discussed bankruptcy further, with Neil providing some information about the government debt helpline for Meg to take home with her.

One of Meg's friends worked close by and she found herself gravitating towards his shop laden with this heavy information.

"Bankruptcy!" Jon said.

"I know, it's insane, isn't it?" she replied.

"It's very drastic," Jon stated.

"I have a lot to think about and he's given me a website to look up, so I'm going home now to do that." Meg said her goodbyes and as she walked home she felt like she was floating about the ground, and everything around her seemed out of focus. She could not believe what she had just heard, bankruptcy, really? It was crazy.

When she got home she looked up the information Neil had given her and started to learn about bankruptcy. After she had slept on the idea, Meg was ready to call the helpline and get even more details about this course of action.

Meg was put through to Christine, and once she had given Christine the breakdown of her debts, she told Meg, "You are the ideal candidate for bankruptcy. You do not own property, a car, have any assets at all in fact. What this means is that you make a very clean break and do not have to pay any of the £30K+ debt back."

Christine had been more than helpful.

How do you tell your parents you are about to go bankrupt?

Meg was slowly coming around to the idea that this was in fact the right thing to do and somehow had to break the news to her parents. Everyone wants their parents to be proud of their achievements, so telling them that your business has failed and you have over 30 grand of debt is hard. Meg knew this was going to be a tough phone call because her Dad's best friend was a retired accountant! As soon as she said the words and 'bankruptcy' hung inside the phone line somewhere between them, her Dad said, "Do you know what, we all feared that was going to happen."

Meg laughed with relief.

"I thought you'd be angry or something, Dad."

"No, Roger said ages ago that bankruptcy was on the cards because you have no assets."

Meg felt like a huge weight had been lifted from her shoulders, but still felt so disappointed that she had messed things up so badly.

"How did I go so wrong though?"

"You mustn't think like that Meg" her Dad assured her. "It wasn't your fault, it was those hard-selling franchise owners who fed you a cock-and-bull story. All you did wrong was fall for their lies, and anyway you weren't the only one, were you?" he said.

This was very true. As it turned out there were about 20 unhappy franchisees who were all in the same boat as her: sold a dream that never materialised, and in huge debt because of it.

They chatted further then said their goodbyes. Meg sat with her head in her hands and cried for the first time since the word bankruptcy had been uttered. She cried because she was relieved, because she was sad, and because she now had the unenviable task of telling her four teachers and all the schools they were working in that the company had gone bust.

Bankrupt on 09/09/09

Things moved pretty quickly once the decision had been made. Meg went to the county court and on the morning of 9th September 2009 was declared bankrupt, along with five others. It was done.

She then had to hand over all her financial documentation for the past five years to the official receiver, who would deal with telling all her creditors that they would not be getting paid, and who would now control all her finances for the next year.

The relief was massive. Meg had stopped answering her landline about two months before because most calls were creditors wanting to be paid. They were deeply unpleasant phone calls, where the person on the other end of the phone had obviously been trained to not take no for an answer.

Now she could answer the phone and happily tell them she was bankrupt and that they needed to speak to her official receiver, and here was the number!

She felt like she could breathe again, and once things started to settle down a bit, Meg could start to think about the future.

Visioning her dreams

She started reading loads more self-help books and practise lots of yogic breathing to calm herself. She was trying to 'go with the flow' and stop fighting with life. Meg had also read lots about the law of attraction and was very aware of how negative thoughts bred even more negative thoughts. She was striving to be positive, healthy and accepting. This was her new philosophy.

Out came her vision board, and she re-evaluated the question she regularly asked herself '*If I could have anything, what would it be?*' and went from there.

Creation

She had been teaching children's yoga for a couple of years now and realised that she really enjoyed it. The franchise business had taken her away from the actual teaching and into an office role, so she definitely wanted to pursue a teaching position. She found an old press release with a picture of herself teaching a kids yoga class, removed the old franchise logo, and stuck it on her vision board. Already she had a focus and knew what one of her goals was.

Meg got started with re-branding herself and chose a name and logo that suited her, and made up a letterhead on her computer. She spent just £14.99 on the rights to use the logo legally, which was the only cost of re-branding.

Now that she had more time she could get into a regular exercise regime and bought some 'boot camp' style DVDs with celebrities in them. She felt more motivated now than she had for the last few years. It was another clean slate.

Manifestation

It was around one month later that Meg bumped into her neighbour Theresa, whom she had never had a conversation with before, in the car park. Both girls had lived in the flats for a few years but never crossed paths before. They struck up a conversation and it turned out Theresa was the deputy headteacher of a local primary school. Meg gushed that she was a children's yoga teacher delivering classes in schools. Theresa sounded interested so Meg suggested she drop off a brochure later. Meg had to admit the brochure looked very professional and happily posted it though Theresa's letterbox that evening.

That conversation translated to around £8,000 worth of work for Meg in local schools over the next few years. Theresa had passed Meg's information to the local School Sports Partnership manager who provided and paid for (government funded) sporting activities in all the schools.

Meg loved the work, loved having no staff and having no boss! She had literally created that opportunity because she'd been very clear about what she wanted.

Chapter Five

Now that all the debts were cleared, Meg had enough money coming in to pay her few bills and eat healthily again. The weight slowly but surely started to come off now that she was much more active and eating fresh food again. She felt settled and was more in tune with herself once more. Life had slowed down so that she could experience each moment, rather than feel like being on a rollercoaster: pushed from side to side and tumbled upside down.

She started to accept little things for what they were, without trying to change anything, everything was as it was supposed to be, and she let go of trying to control everything.

She had been so stressed with the franchise business and the lead up to the bankruptcy, that in contrast, her life now was great. She was eternally grateful to have the ability to be grateful!

Tara and Grace

She decided to get two kittens from her local sanctuary and popped in one Sunday to see if there were two cats available. The lovely lady took her into the young kitten area and showed her four litters. All the kittens in two of the litters were reserved, and only one from each other available. She had asked for two and there were only two left, so she took them. She felt like they were just meant to be with her.

Meg was nervous that because they weren't real sisters they wouldn't get along with each other and fight. She was trying to go with the flow and stop worrying because this was her new way of thinking. Her kittens would be fine because they were both meant to be with her.

She really felt for them the first couple of days as they gingerly checked out their new home and each other, and jumped every time she came into the room or put the telly on.

Grace was black with white paws and belly, and Tara was white with black patches. About four or five days after their arrival, Meg returned home from work and quietly peeked into the living room where she was holding them until they were old enough to go out. The two kittens were curled up together in a tight warm ball on the sofa!

It was the cutest thing that Meg had ever seen, and as she watched them peacefully sleeping she thought how they had just reinforced her 'everything will be OK if you just let it' philosophy. Her heart felt like it was about to burst with love for Grace and Tara, and for life!

She was learning to trust the process and stop fighting with life, instead flowing in harmony with it. But how could she maintain this feeling, as it seemed to be so fleeting whenever it appeared.

I love the highs but hate the lows

It was great to feel these highs, but unfortunately they were usually followed by some bad news or a really huge bill just when her bank balance was at an all time low, and she came crashing down from her love of life back to 'Why is this happening to me?"

Meg yearned for more balance in her life rather than the constant high and low energy that so exhausted her. She never knew what her mood was going to be.

Through her children's yoga training she had experienced a little meditation before, but when she saw a programme about the science of meditation on TV it rang a bell in her head and sparked her into action.

Chapter Five

Finding the present moment

Tibetan monks had been wired up to machines and put through MRI scans to measure and study their brain patterns.

The programme was amazing and showed how brain activity shifted during meditation to a calmer part of the brain and away from where we hold stress, which meant the practitioner felt calmer, happier and more in control of their lives. Meg started to research the subject. What she found amazed her: the brain actually changed dramatically over time with consistent (and not necessarily long) sessions of meditation. She learnt that people like the Dalai Lama who meditated at great length everyday were not even capable of negative and harmful emotions like hate, anger and fear! Which perhaps explains the Dalai Lama's compassion towards the Chinese government who have occupied his country for over 50 years.

The more information Meg gathered, the more interested she became and soon had downloaded some CDs and had many books. At first she tried to meditate alone at home but found it really hard to 'switch off'. Books and research told her this was normal. She learnt that the mind is like any other muscle in the body and needs to be exercised. Everyone knows that you need to exercise your body to be physically fit, but Meg hadn't thought before about how her mind was supposed to be kept healthy too.

The CDs told her to sit quietly and comfortably and keep her back straight. Then close the eyes and watch the breath coming in and out, keeping the attention in the present moment.

But that was Meg's problem, her mind just didn't seem to want to stay in one place. Instead it was off all over the place, delving into her worries, problems and plans.

"Rest assured," said the books. "What you are experiencing is normal."

She kept at it because she did sometimes experience the odd gap in between her thoughts, and it was very nice.

Meditation class

It was all very well meditating at home, but Meg knew the time was coming that she would like to have a teacher who she could ask questions. There were certain things that she didn't know whether she was doing right, and it would be good to meet others who were doing the same thing. She started researching online for local groups and soon came across a teacher who had tons of experience and held three classes a week in her local studio. She sent an email and got herself booked onto the Tuesday evening class.

The studio was very inviting with a luxuriously soft carpet, dimmed lights, candles everywhere and incense burning. Meg felt instantly at ease as she got herself a cushion from the pile, and a blanket. The teacher was a petite woman with kind, knowing eyes.

"Are you Meg?" she came over and asked.

"Hi, yes, and you must be Jo."

"Yes, it's really nice to meet you and welcome to the group." Jo continued, "You can sit against the wall to give your back support, or sit a little bit away from it if you want. It's good to sit on one or two cushions which will get your back really straight. Have you done any meditation before?"

"Only at home. I've been teaching myself from books, and have a few CDs that I listen to," Meg told her.

"That's great, you will be familiar with some of the techniques that I use, and I think you will really enjoy the dynamics of meditating in a group." Jo sounded so positive that Meg couldn't wait to get started.

There were nine people in the studio and at 8pm on the

dot, Jo turned down the lights completely and started to play a Tibetan singing bowl. The sound was haunting and you couldn't help yourself but stay with it until you could hear it no longer.

"Start to watch your breathing," Jo was speaking very softly, "noticing your natural rhythm tonight." She paused and played a different singing bowl this time. It was a higher pitch but equally hypnotic.

"Breathing in and breathing out," Jo was saying, "let go of your thoughts, and be fully present in this moment."

The 30 minutes was a mixture of Jo reminding them to come back to the present moment, playing the singing bowls and complete silence.

Meg couldn't believe how quickly 30 minutes had gone! It seemed more like 10! Wow, it was so much easier here in the group.

Jo turned the lights on gently and everyone stretched and said Namaste. Jo asked if anyone had any questions or anything they wanted to share with the group.

"That went really quickly," said a woman called Serena.

"Yes it whizzed by tonight," agreed a young girl called Wendy.

Meg kept quiet but was secretly really pleased that everyone else also thought the session had gone super quick. That meant that what she had experienced tonight wasn't a fluke.

Everyone started to stand up and put their cushions away. They seemed to be a friendly lot.

"How was that Meg?" Jo had made a beeline for her.

"That was amazing. Completely different to what I've been doing at home."

"Yes, you will find that. It's much easier to let go of your thoughts here in this environment, but it's extremely important that you also practise at home daily. Even if it's just for five or ten minutes, it's not so much the length of time but the regularity." Jo stressed.

"OK, I can definitely do that, and I'll be back next week" she said.

"Perfect," Jo replied.

Getting into a good habit

It said in the books that you should practice at the same time every day. Meg loved the beginning of the day and often got up early to enjoy the peace, quiet and stillness of the morning, so decided that she would meditate for ten minutes as soon as she arose.

It was a great way to start the day. She made herself a cup of tea after her ten minutes' practice and sat reflecting on how different her meditation was each day. Sometimes Meg's mind was all over the place like a wild horse not wanting to be tamed, but other times it was like flicking a switch and boom! ...her mind was peaceful.

The real work, though, was learning not to judge yourself too harshly, because even the days that the mind is crazy you are still meditating and still changing the brain.

It's all part of the practice to accept the changes from day to day. Jo talked about the parallel that our meditation practice had with the rest of our lives and how it's all linked. She said if you could accept your 'good' and 'bad' practice then you will be more capable of dealing with the 'good' times and 'bad' times in your everyday life.

"You are training your brain to accept situations and go with the flow," she would say sometimes during or after the sessions "When you fully accept and give up the fight, then you are free to enjoy what each moment brings."

Meg enjoyed these snippets of information that Jo gave,

and sometimes she would talk to the group at length after their class.

"We don't meditate to become good at meditation, we meditate because it has a direct positive effect on every area of our lives. We are dropping down underneath the layers of thoughts to a deeper, quieter, more peaceful place where we learn to let go of *doing* and just *be*. Then from this *being* place we can accept, and when we can accept our meditation practice, then we can accept our current relationships, health, job and family.

"It also makes us feel more in control, so if any of the above needs changing we realise we are in fact in a position to make those changes, and not feel powerless or lost."

It was really interesting and after a few months Meg realised she was now regularly meditating for longer than the planned 10 minutes. It was becoming much more natural, the time was passing by quicker, and she was definitely noticing subtle changes in her behaviour and moods. She wasn't as snappy and just seemed generally more content with her lot.

Jo was doing an intensive day-long course at the weekend which Meg was really looking forward to, it was four hours of meditation rather than the usual 30 minutes, lovely!

Intensive stuff

There were just six of them at Jo's studio for the intensive course, which was going to be part discussion and part meditation. There were three themes: acceptance; trust; flow. Jo assured them all that they were going to feel really happy at the end of the day.

They started with a basic meditation on the breath and imagining they were swimming in the ocean. Jo's voice was cool and calm:

"You're swimming in the warm ocean and it feels great, and don't worry if you can't swim because you can within this visualisation..." Jo fell silent for a while allowing them to really imagine they were in the water, then she continued,

"Feel the water, and how it pushes you around.......What is the temperature of the water? What can you see? Can you smell or taste the water? What does it sound like? You are using your senses to really make the visualisation as real as possible.......Then the wind picks up and the water gets a little choppy, now it's getting really rough. Lets imagine that we drop down under the surface of the water and descend towards the bottom. Don't worry, you can breathe under water in this visualisation.

As we reach the ocean floor we sit and enjoy the peace and quiet down here, and look up and see that the surface is still turbulent, that the waves are still crashing. But we are not now affected by this turbulence, we have created a space between it and us......

We can see it, but are not affected by it, and this is exactly what we are doing in meditation. We are going to a different, deeper part of the brain, and are able to access happiness here, peace here and contentment here.......

Our thoughts are still at the surface, we are not trying to push them away, but we leave them alone, let them be, and settle into this deeper part of our minds........."

Jo spoke for a bit, and then stayed silent, allowing each of them to rest their busy minds and fully immerse themselves in the visualisation. The analogy was great because it really showed Meg what she should be doing. When she had first started she realised she'd been pushing her thoughts away, and in effect fighting with her mind. Now, through this analogy particularly, she understood better what this thing called meditation was.

Thoughts came into her mind, yes, but she simply acknowledged them and let them go, not pursuing them or getting caught up in them. Obviously sometimes she did get pulled away, and as soon as she became aware that she'd gone off somewhere into fantasy, she gently reminded herself to come back to the ocean floor and her breath. It was all about being in the present moment.

At the end of the 30 minutes Jo started to talk again,

"Now look up towards the surface of the water and see the waves and the movement again. We will start to swim back up and bring ourselves out of our meditation. We rejoin our world with a new perspective, and bring some of the peace and contentment back up with us."

They then spent the next hour discussing their experience and asking questions.

Hold your awareness with the sound of the gong

Their next meditation was on sound. Jo had many singing bowls and also a gong, which was really loud. They all got comfortable and Jo began:

"Start to become aware of sounds you can hear outside the room. You might hear a car go past, birds singing, a plane in the sky…" She allowed them time to tune in to what was going on outside for a while. Then she continued,

"Now bring your attention to the sounds inside the room: my voice; the singing bowls; the sounds that you or someone else might be making." She paused for a few minutes and left them in silence other than the occasional sound of a singing bowl.

"As we rest our minds on the support of sound, we try to have no judgements of 'good' and 'bad' sounds. The sounds are simply going to remind us to return to the present moment, so you hear something and let it go, don't think, 'Ah, what a lovely bird singing,' and get caught up in how wonderful it is to hear the birds. And equally when a car alarm goes off try not to get caught up in how annoying the sound is. Use both types of sound in the same way to bring you back into the present moment."

Again she paused for a while to allow the group to try the technique. Meg definitely found it difficult to not judge the sounds and label them either 'pleasant' or 'unpleasant'. She was trying to view them all in a similar manner.

Jo played the different singing bowls and fell completely silent again for a while. Then she hit one of the bowls just once and asked them to follow the sound until they could hear it no more. Once it was quiet again she hit it again, and again they followed the sound until it was gone. This went on for about 10 minutes and Meg found it amazing how this sound held your attention. There were literally no thoughts in her head.

After this Jo then started to play the gong. It was a two metre high upright instrument hanging from a stand and was played with two felt covered batons. As she sat in front of it, it towered over Jo, and she started to play it very softly. Then louder, then louder still, the sound like waves washing over them. This is actually called a "gong wash" or "gong bath" because the sound waves do wash over and through your body.

It felt really good! Just when Meg thought Jo had played it as loud as was possible, she went louder still, then soft, then loud. Up and down. Strong and soft. Loud and quiet. It was beautiful and filled her head with sound so that there was no room for thoughts, and the only way Meg could describe it was like an orgasm!

Meg loved it and could feel how she was being energised by

it. Jo had said that the sound waves move through your body breaking down blockages whether they be physical (pain and disease), mental (addictions), or emotional (anger and fear, etc.), and Meg could appreciate how. It was like the sound penetrated every cell in her body.

Jo had been silent for a few minutes and now gently nudged them out of their meditation:

"Start to move your fingers and toes and stretch any way you need to. Then sit comfortably and bring your hands together in a prayer position at your chest. Look down towards your heart and thank yourself for your practice, for giving yourself this precious time to let go of the outside world and go within. Namaste."

She always said similar words at the end to close the session. Meg opened her eyes and looked down at her shaking body. The gong had really affected her and it felt great.

"How was that?" asked Jo.

"Amazing," said Claire. "There was no room for thoughts once the gong got going."

"Yes, it's extremely powerful, and not everyone likes it." explained Jo.

Everyone in this group, however, had really enjoyed it.

"It is so different from the calm and peaceful first meditation that we did this morning," piped up Meg, "and I'm shaking. Look!" she held out her hands and showed the group. Others had had a similar experience, in fact they were all buzzing!

"How wonderful!" exclaimed Jo "That was a much longer meditation than we normally do because I wanted you to really get into the gong. We were sitting for 45 minutes."

"Sitting" was the term used when one did the formal practice, and Jo explained that when the formal sitting finished, the practitioner carried on with the meditation practice in everything that they did. The qualities of acceptance, trust, flow and letting go carry through into our relationships, work, family life and health. One became more mindful and this was the theme to the last meditation of the day.

They discussed their findings further over tea and some delicious chocolate that Jo had made.

The body scan

Jo started the final session.

"So for this meditation we are going to lay down on our backs with a very straight back, with our arms out to the side, palms facing up. Close your eyes."

Everyone got themselves organised with cushions under their heads and blankets over them, and Jo continued, "Become aware of your breathing and your body as a whole." She paused for a few minutes for them to do this, then:

"We are going to bring our awareness up and through the body one part at a time and really try and feel how that part is today. This exercise is about accepting what we find, not having an expectation about it, and not judging it.

"If we've had an injury or experienced pain in a certain part of our body in the past, we must not bring that expectation of pain to this practice because the pain may not even be there, but we can project it there if we're not careful."

"We may come across pain, discomfort, an itch, heat, cold or even nothing at all. There are no right or wrong answers, your experience in this moment is all that matters. Let's start with the toes of your left foot, starting with the big toe…then the second toe…then the middle toe, feeling the contact that each individual toe has with the one next to it. Now come to the fourth toe…and the little toe… Move your attention to the sole of your left foot, if you have a sock on or a blanket over you you may feel the contact your foot has with it…

bring your attention now around the sides of the foot, and then to the top of the foot…come into the ankle now."

Jo moved slowly like this with silent gaps in between each body part, all the way up the left leg and then repeated the same thing on the right side. It was so detailed and Meg experienced different sensations in different parts of her body. Her attention drifted off to wondering what her kittens were up to this Saturday afternoon, then to what she'd like to eat for dinner, then to the contents of her fridge. She didn't know how long she'd strayed away for, or if she'd actually fallen asleep, but Jo was now saying:

"Perhaps you can feel a warmth in the palms of your hands…and a heaviness in the backs of your hands as they rest on the floor…"

Had she really missed her whole torso?!

"…now moving up both arms to the elbows…upper arms…shoulders and shoulder blades…now aware of how the neck feels and the throat…up into the jaw."

Yes! She'd missed from the top of the right leg to the palms of her hands, bugger!

"…are the muscles in the face tensed or relaxed?"

Jo continued up, up, up,

"all the way around the back of the head, feeling the weight of your head resting on the floor."

Had she fallen asleep? Or just daydreamed?

She didn't know and felt quite frustrated. Then Jo was saying:

"Start to move your fingers and toes and stretch your body. Roll onto your right side into a foetal position. Breathe there for two breaths, and then push yourself up to sitting with your head coming up last, protect your head, then bring your hands together in a prayer position at your chest and look down towards your heart. Thank yourself for taking the time to meet each part of your body and accept what you have found wholly. Namaste."

She then asked, "Does anyone have any questions?"

"I think I fell asleep and I'm really annoyed with myself," Meg confessed.

"Don't worry" Jo smiled "It's very easy to do. I can't do the body scan in the afternoon as I always fall asleep! I have to do it in the morning." She added "You must accept that falling asleep was what you needed to do today, please don't feel annoyed or disappointed. It is all part of our practice. Next time if you feel yourself start to drift off, open your eyes and look up at the ceiling."

The ceiling in Jo's studio was draped in material and very pleasant to look at so Meg thought this was a good idea. They finished their day together discussing how they could be more mindful in everyday life.

"You could choose a task that you do everyday, like brushing your teeth or hair, or eating breakfast or lunch, and do it without thinking about anything else. We hardly ever do this normally, we are always daydreaming," suggested Jo.

"Yeah, I am always watching the TV when I eat," another student shared, "so I don't even really taste what I'm eating, especially if I'm watching something really interesting."

Everyone agreed that eating and TV watching was not a good combination, and they all vowed to do less of it. Meg usually ate lunch by herself so it was feasible for her to have one mindful meal alone per day.

How amazing would it be to always feel this good

Meg had loads of tips and methods that she would take home from the intensive course, and she felt very positive. She was really pleased she had come. The other participants were nice too, she'd only met a couple of them at the Tuesday evening class before so it was good to meet more like-minded people.

She thanked Jo and said her goodbyes. She felt much calmer and everything seemed to be slower. It was a good feeling, everything seemed to be under control, and she was going to make that feeling last for as long as possible. She'd been assured that if she continued to practice *formally* and *informally* daily then she could sustain this feeling. How wonderful would it be to always feel in control of your life!

Jo had told them that gradually over time the balance had shifted for her towards feeling in control and happy more and more. It took time but was very possible for anyone, and this was what Meg was going to work towards.

Over the coming months and years, Meg did feel the balance shifting and her life becoming more stable and grounded. Subtle but perceivable changes that made life flow more easily and not knock her so hard.

Meditation was now a massive support and Meg couldn't imagine being without it.

Stabilising

Jo was running a weekend retreat soon and had one room left which Meg decided she was going to take. She had enjoyed the intensive day so much, and knew a whole weekend of yoga and meditation would take her closer to where she wanted to be. In fact, she felt that she was already exactly where she wanted to be, the retreat would help secure her there!

Chapter Six

The Retreat
A Big Chunk of Getting Unstuck

"Imagine a hot tub for the mind. That is what meditation is; it can bathe your mind in relaxing thoughts"
Eknath Easwaran

In Transit...

Grant

The Audi A5 2.0 TDI was one thing I didn't relinquish in my 'new' life as it is such a pleasure to drive. It is literally purring down the M11 effortlessly and almost seems to know where it is going. Both the car and myself can't wait to get to the house and see Jo again. I've not seen her since I came to this same retreat a few years ago, and so much has happened that I can't wait to tell her about. She inspired me to follow my dream and I can't wait to see where her retreat takes me this time.

As a yoga teacher myself it's a massive treat to become the student for a whole weekend. I'm used to being at the front and doing the talking and guiding, so for me I'm looking forward to listening and learning. I know that it will always be like this: a period of learning, followed by a period of teaching; and so the cycle continues.

My right foot lovingly plays with the accelerator pedal and even though I left home later than planned I still arrive right on time and before anyone else.

"Grant!" Jo exclaims.

"Oh, Jo, it's brilliant to be back in this stunning house, I have loads to tell you about India, thanks so much for all the advice you gave me. I had the most amazing time."

"And are you teaching now?"

"Yes, I'm teaching full time and loving it. It's so what I'm meant to be doing with my life."

"That's just amazing Grant" Jo says with a big smile as she knew exactly what he meant.

Meg

I drive happily at the national speed limit, meandering through flat and vast Norfolk, and find it almost amusing when aggressive and impatient drivers feel frustrated when stuck behind me. I know they drive up close and try to intimidate me into driving faster, but that is just never going to happen. Deep down I feel sorry for them and the impatience they feel to get everywhere in record time shouting at, and intimidating whoever gets in their path. What a horrible way to live!

My continual and consistent meditation practice has really slowed down my inner and outer world and created space like a buffer. I feel protected from negative outside influence and the buffer allows me to make conscious choices when bombarded with the everyday stress of work, family and staying healthy.

The drive takes just over three hours, and when I pull into

the gravel drive there are already two cars parked up.

The house is gorgeous and grand and I can't believe I'm actually here. As I get my case from the boot I see Jo at the door waving.

"Hi Jo, how are you?"

"Great thanks, Meg, you?"

"Brilliant, and so pleased to be here."

"How was your journey?"

"Fine, no problems."

"Come on in and I'll show you to your room and put the kettle on."

Jo leads me through the house and up two flights of stairs to my room. It is huge with an amazing view, and what looks like the cosiest bed I've ever seen.

Sam

I'm excited as I look out the window and watch the countryside flash past as the train tears towards Kings Lynn station. This is something that I would never have done for myself when I was still with Bobby, and it feels great to give myself a whole weekend for just *me*. I can imagine him whinging about the cost of the weekend or who was going to cook his dinner while I'm away!

I've only ever spent one hour at a time with Jo in our coaching sessions and the time always whizzes by so quickly that I am really looking forward to being around her all weekend. She is always so positive and optimistic which rubs off on everyone around her. I have to admit, though, to being slightly apprehensive about the yoga which I've never done before, but we'll see. I'm also really intrigued to meet Jo's husband who is apparently doing all the cooking over the weekend, and you never know there could be some fit men attending!

I'm soon exiting the station and hailing a cab. The house is only a few miles away and we arrive quickly with little traffic.

The front door is open and I enter the most beautiful house I have ever seen. The décor is all cream and beige and we have been notified in advance to bring slippers as the owner likes you to leave your shoes at the entrance.

To the immediate right is our practice room where Jo has laid out a mat for each of us and has candles placed all around the room. I am immediately at ease, and a sense of calm descends around me. I know I am going to enjoy the weekend.

Jo walks down the long corridor from where some of the other attendees are having tea in the kitchen.

"Hi Sam, how are you?"

"Great thanks, Jo. This house is amazing!"

"Yeah it's got a really lovely feel to it, it's a happy house!"

"How many of us are coming this weekend Jo?"

"There are five of you, plus Dominic and myself, so very intimate. Come on, let's get you a cup of tea and I'll introduce you to who's here already."

Rob

Unfortunately I couldn't get out of work as early as I'd hoped so I'm now on the 3.15pm train instead of the 2.15pm train out of Kings Cross.

Annabel had seriously asked me if I thought everyone would be drinking wine in the evenings. I hope and suspect that I will be sharing my weekend with others enjoying sobriety.

I've now not had a drink for 94 days and am looking forward to celebrating 100 days by going out for a meal with the wife. She had joked that we could share a bottle of wine to celebrate but I actually didn't find that very funny. She thinks I've turned boring now that I don't drink, but the reality is that this is the real me.

This weekend has come at a brilliant time, and I hope to cement my meditation practice with extended and more regular sessions. I've never done yoga before and I have to say I'm quite looking forward to giving it a go, as I've never been into any type of exercise, so it will be good for me I think.

There are plenty of taxis at the station.

I let myself in and hear Jo's music playing close by and someone laughing in a different part of the house. Then the smell of incense hits my nose and it is the regular Tibetan brand that Jo burns at my meditation class in her studio.

The house is on a very grand scale with a library on the left and where we will be doing our classes I guess on the right. I walk further down the hallway and see a fancy dining room on the left with about 20 places all laid out formally with huge candles on the table and chandeliers hanging above. To the right is what looks like a home entertainment room with huge comfy sofas and massive projector. Very cool!

Finally at the end of the long hallway are the stairs to the left and the kitchen to the right. This is where all the laughter is coming from, and as I enter I see five people sitting around a table drinking hot drinks. Jo jumps up and bounds toward me.

"I didn't hear you come in, Rob!"

"A cab just dropped me off."

"How was your journey?"

"Seamless, once I could finally get out of work."

"Great, and how are you?"

"Happy to be here. I need this and I'm so pleased I've taken the time for myself."

"That's great Rob. Now come and meet everyone and have something to drink as we are nearly ready to start our first session. We're just waiting for one more person to arrive."

Joss

I'm late as usual and now stuck in London's Friday rush hour traffic. The first session starts at 5pm and, damn! I'm not going to make it on time.

England is so hectic compared to my serene Thai beach existence, and I have to say I really need a break, if I can just get out of this traffic!

The past few weeks since I've been back have been a major shock to the system and thrown me completely off balance. I so need this weekend away to restore calm and clarity.

I put my foot down as soon as I'm able to and thankfully the traffic melts away as I escape London's madness.

I have high expectations of this weekend. I don't want to be feeling as I do right now, I seem to have completely lost my mojo since leaving Thailand and am quite literally all over the place. I've also never met Jo so I hope I like her and we get along OK. I hate feeling apprehensive but there are so many unknown factors. I really hope this is not a disaster.

I seem to be making up some time but as I get nearer to the venue I am feeling more and more nervous.

I arrive only half an hour late in the end and drive into a very grand residence and park the car. There is someone at the door, which is a nice welcome.

"Hi, I'm Jo. You must be Joss."

"Yes, hi, Jo. Wow, this house is awesome!"

"I know, can you imagine living here?!"

"It would be amazing to! Sorry I'm late but the traffic was horrible."

"That's fine, Joss, we haven't got started yet so you've not missed anything."

The interior is as gorgeous as the exterior, and I feel relaxed automatically somehow. Maybe meeting Jo and seeing that she's very nice, or the vibe of the house, or the music and incense I'm aware of in the air. I don't know why, just that I feel like I've made a huge sigh at the front door and left all that stress and anticipation in my car. I'm not going to let it come in with me.

I meet the rest of the group who are all in the kitchen and Jo leads me to my room on the first floor. It is huge. Bigger than the whole two bedroom flat I am currently staying in in London, and there are three of us living there! I have a four-poster bed with material laced around the frame, a chaise longue, massive wardrobe and a big bay window to look out at the rolling Norfolk plains. The bathroom is huge, too, with a separate shower and bath. Crazy big!

Jo invites me to join everyone else in the practice room as soon as I'm ready, and when she leaves I collapse on my gorgeous bed and wonder if this deluxe duvet is going to allow me to go anywhere tonight. Then I notice something on the bed and see that I have to fill out a questionnaire numbering how stressed I'm feeling and what emotions I have in this moment. I note that I must go through the same process at the end of the retreat to highlight the changes that may occur. I'm sure I will be feeling very different in 48 hours time, and make my way downstairs to the yoga room. I glance around the room at my fellow retreatants. Everyone looks pretty frazzled and like they are in dire need of some relaxation.

Opening meditation

Jo begins, "Please choose one of the mats which you will use over the whole weekend. It's good to have your own space that you can keep coming back to."

"Sit comfortably, cross-legged if possible, with hands resting on your knees with your first fingers and thumbs together to create a 'mudra'. Backs are straight and eyes closed. Become aware of your breathing and start to calm the mind down."

"Scan your attention from the top of your head, all the way down your body and become aware of how each part of your body feels right now. When you have reached your toes try to feel the body as a whole. Remember how you feel now at the beginning of our weekend together as I will ask you to do the same thing in our closing meditation."

Jo pauses and allows the students time to do this.

"Become aware now of how easy that was for your mind to stay in the present moment. Did you wander off into the past or future? Or was your mind strong and steady? It is most probable that whatever your experience is tonight will change, grow and become more stable."

"I want you to fully feel your experience right now, so that you can be conscious of how the weekend evolves."

The group moves on to some diaphragmatic breathing and then onto the physical asanas. The session is slow and mindful of posture, ensuring the spine is always straight and supported. The physical practice ends this evening hanging upside down on an inversion table. Jo advises how this is done,

"OK, Meg, hook your feet under the bar and make sure the bar is secured tightly, so that the table part is behind you. Then hold on to the side rails as the table moves backwards.

That's it! How does it feel?"

"Great, Jo! All the blood is rushing to my head, I love it!"

Meg's feet are now in the air, and her head down near the floor. Gravity is pulling her spine straight and she is receiving the most amazing intensive stretch all through her body. This is excellent for the back specifically, to realign and strengthen, and the extra blood to the head, brain and face has an all-round feeling of relaxation.

Jo performs a Gong Wash to finish the session. Everyone lays down with a blanket over them, as Jo starts to play the gong softly, then louder, and louder still. Back and forth, strong and soft, powerful and supportive.

The difference in everyone after just the first session is amazing! Their faces already show that they have all chilled out!

Dominic's fabulous cooking

They all file into the grand dining room to await the first meal of tofu Thai coconut curry, rice and steamed veggies. Dominic loves cooking and it shows, the food is delicious!

Everyone chats over dinner as this is the first time the retreatants have had to properly talk to each other.

Jo gives them all the weekend's timetable which includes three sessions of yoga and meditation per day, plus one coaching session each. Everything is optional so you can choose to have a lie-in if you don't want to get up for the early meditation!

The coaching sessions are designed to give everyone some formal one-to-one time with Jo to discuss personal goals and challenges. This is an important part of the weekend so that the student is very clear about the direction in which they are travelling.

Visioning your future

After dinner they move into the living room, which houses a number of huge sofas which everyone melts into. Jo is discussing vision boards with the group and explaining that they are a great way of reminding you of your intended path, and keeping you on course.

"Life has a habit of pulling you in different directions which makes it easy to get lost, distracted or disinterested in your goals," she tells them, "The vision board brings you straight back to your dreams, your purpose and your intentions.

"There are large bits of paper, magazines, scissors and glue. I suggest you flick through the magazines and cut out any pictures that inspire you."

Proof it works

Jo then shows everyone a picture of her sister and brother-in-law looking very loved up and happy together. "This is the picture that I placed on my vision board and hoped to manifest a relationship as loving as theirs. Five years later I went to a friend's wedding with my new partner, Dominic, and a few weeks later the friend sent me some pictures of the wedding through the post. Among them was an almost identical picture of Dominic and me as the one I had on my vision board! I had made that dream a reality and we later went on to get married."

Jo then pulls out the photo of her and Dominic and both photos are passed around the group.

Joss and Rob have never even heard of a vision board but are both willing to give it a go.

After everything she'd been through with Bobby, and her subsequent time alone, Sam was definitely ready to find a healthy, stable relationship. She starts shifting through the magazines for inspiring photos of hot men.

Jo stands up and as she stretches and yawns, says:

"So the paper, magazines, scissors and all the stuff for the vision boards will be left here all weekend so that you can work on them whenever you need to. Take them to your room if you want or work on it down here, it's up to you. I'm off to bed now as we have an early start in the morning. Meet you in the practice room at 8am for sun salutations and meditation."

"Night Jo and Dominic" said Meg, Joss and Rob one after the other.

"Anyone need anything before I go?" asked Jo. "And please help yourself to hot or cold drinks at any time. And you have the fruit and snacks I've left out if you're hungry."

"Yeah, I think we're all good, Jo," replied Grant. "You get yourself to bed."

"Thanks! Night all!"

Saturday's timetable

Saturday starts with 20 sun salutations followed by a 30 minute meditation. The sun salutations get the body and mind into gear, and fire up your day. They really do wake you up and get you focused. The meditation further focuses everyone and finishes with a light playing of the gong. Everyone has slept pretty well, and are now buzzing from the mornings practice.

Breakfast is a buffet of cereals, toast, smoothie, and fruit with yoghurt. Some down time follows and a few go for a walk, while others chill out with their vision boards or in their rooms.

The next session is before lunch and once again everyone joins together in the fabulous practice room.

If You Could Have Anything...

"It's time for a backbend class," Jo tells the group "which lifts and opens our energy, and we will finish off with a very loud gong wash!"

Jo leads them through some meditation, then Kabalabhati breathing before they start on the physical postures.

"Each backbend that we perform today will be slightly harder than the preceding one, meaning that Urdvah Dhanurasana (wheel pose) will be our grand finale.

"So let's lie down on our tummies and bring the hands under our shoulders and bring the head just off the floor but still looking down towards the floor. On your inhale lengthen your spine and on the exhale lift up slightly. Make sure you tighten your buttocks as you do this to protect your back."

The group progress through the postures with Jo encouraging them to ask questions when they encounter something they don't understand.

"You must ask if it doesn't make sense, otherwise what's the point in doing it!" She'd say.

They finish off their session of backbends with some forward bends to balance the effects, then Jo plays the gong much louder than the previous night.

Everyone walks out with wide eyes and big smiles.

As it is summer, Dominic has prepared a cold lunch of rustic bread, hummus, dips, cheese and salad. There is more fruit smoothie and fresh lemon and mint to liven up tap water. It is delicious and everyone eats, chats, and gets to know each other better. Everyone is here ultimately for the same reason, and enjoy like-minded company.

The individual coaching sessions will start in an hour and all the retreatants have an allotted time.

So what is your dream?

Grant is first and eager to get going.

"So, Grant, is there any particular area that you'd like to discuss today?" Jo starts to probe.

"Well, yes, I've been teaching for a while now, and things seem to be a bit stuck." Grant started to explain some more, "I have a partnership with a gym owner and I'm mainly working with her, which is great, but I think I might need something else."

"And what direction would you like to go in Grant?"

"I don't know really" he looks downward, and Jo tries a different angle.

"What is your dream job, if you could have anything?"

Grant now looks upwards as he thinks it through "Ehm… well… I would really like *my own* studio one day."

Jo jumps on this information, "That's great, Grant."

"But I can't imagine how I could ever do that. It would cost so much money, and what if it failed?"

"Grant, you're doing what most people do, not believing that their dreams can come true and closing down all available possibilities. Think about all that you have achieved over the last few years. You followed your heart, and the universe did the rest. You opened up and allowed your dream to materialise because you believed it could. Now do the same again."

Jo is really excited for him and knows he just needs a tiny bit of guidance to push him through the door of doubt.

Grant has his eyes closed and is visualising how his studio will look. He imagines his logo on the door, and the smell of his favourite incense throughout. Soft music plays and he has a full yoga class. He opens his eyes and laughs, "Got it!"

He closes his eyes again as he now doesn't want to leave the ambiance of his vision.

"So, try to be with the feeling you have right now, as often as you can, so that you are attracting to you that exact same energy that is needed to actually make it happen. You have just planted a seed and now you need to water that seed regularly with belief that it can happen. *If you do believe* then the seed will begin to grow. BUT, you will not see anything to start off with because the seed is still underground. This is where lots of people give up, think it's not working, and go back to their old negative way of thinking. *If you don't believe* then the seed will wither and die and so too will your dream before it even got started."

Grant can see that it makes sense big time, he'd done it before, and had made things happen in his life because he'd had no doubt that they were going to happen.

Don't water your weeds

"So, Grant, using the exact same analogy, we must keep our minds away from negative thoughts. If we ponder something upsetting constantly, then we are watering and growing more of it. We must start with the awareness that this is a universal law that we are governed by, just like the law of gravity. Once we understand that whatever is in our heads is multiplied, then it gets much easier to have the right things there to supply us with support, love, happiness and abundance."

"I am trying, Jo!" Grant replies.

Jo continues, "I often use the image of your brain being like a magnet and the magnet attracting the same thing to it. You don't question why or how this happens, you just accept that it does, and so too with your thoughts."

Grant leaves the session with thoughts filling his head of the direction he now sees himself travelling.

Chapter Six

Looking for love

Sam is next. She sits down and Jo asks her, "How are you finding the weekend so far Sam?"

"I'm really enjoying it, and the direction I already feel I'm finding."

"Is there any area in your life that you'd like to talk about, Sam?"

"In all honesty Jo, every area of my life is a mess!"

"What's the most important area to you right now, though?"

"A good wholesome loving relationship."

"OK, great, and what qualities are you looking for in this relationship, Sam?"

"Ehm….kindness, softness, understanding, love, support… all the things my ex didn't give me."

"Well, at least you know what you will never accept in a relationship again!"

"Yes."

"You've learnt a lot from that relationship, Sam, and you're now free to find someone who can give you everything that you long for and deserve."

"I can't wait! I've seen what a great relationship you and Dominic have, and that's the kind of support and acceptance of *me* that I'm looking for."

"Ah, that's sweet! OK, what you need to do is write down all the qualities of your ideal mate, and don't leave anything out. His personality, his looks, age, kids, everything. You are making an order, so put as much detail as possible on your list as if you were going to the supermarket!"

"OK, I can do that."

"Write it out, get it on your vision board, and just know that he is on his way to you. He is tying up his loose ends to make himself available to you, just as you are doing everything you can to be ready for him."

"Wow, I can do that."

"He is out there Sam, don't you worry, the man (or woman) who will have all the qualities that are important to you. Sam leaves the session bouncing off the walls, and bounds up the stairs and into her room to make the list.

Learning to get fitter and healthier

Next up is Rob.

"How are you getting on with your vision board?" Jo asks.

"Well, I've not done anything like this before and I don't really know where to start, to be honest."

"OK, well, is there an area of your life that you'd like to change or improve?"

"The thing is, I'm three months into giving up booze, and actually feeling really good about myself."

"That's fantastic, Rob."

"I didn't think it was going to be this easy so have to say I'm really pleased with myself!"

"Wow, that must feel amazing! Can you imagine anything else that might also make you feel better about yourself?"

Rob looks around the room as he's thinking, picking up ideas and discarding them in his mind. Finally there seems to be something worth holding on to.

"One really positive effect I've noticed from not drinking has been having more energy and generally feeling much healthier, and I love it. So I think I might finally be ready to join a gym and start exercising."

"Is exercise something you don't normally participate in then, Rob?"

"I've always found an excuse not to!" he laughs.

"OK, well this is another positive step forward, because as soon as you start making your heart work harder, the more energy you're going to have."

"Brilliant, well, that's definitely something I want to start up."

"Why don't you write that down as something you're going to do when you return home from this weekend, and maybe include it on your vision board?"

"OK."

"What else, Rob?"

"Along the same lines, I really enjoyed the smoothie that Dominic made at breakfast. I think I could eat healthier food which would be good for me and my family."

"Great. Do you have a blender at home?"

"No."

"Why don't you write that on your list too?"

Rob leaves the session feeling motivated to get healthier and fitter.

Letting go

Meg comes into the room next and sits down. She is smiling. "I have been doing my vision board for the last few years, Jo, and think they're great."

"Brill, and how have you got on?"

"With quite a lot of success, actually."

"That's great, Meg. Yes, they really do help to keep you focused. Is there something particular you'd like to focus on today?"

"There is actually. The bankruptcy was the best decision I ever made as it allowed me to let go of all that stress and move onwards. I felt like I was shedding a skin."

"Wow, Meg, that's fantastic, what a great feeling."

"Yes, it was, but it's so easy to slip back into feeling stuck again. I learnt such a big lesson of how liberating letting go of the past is, and I want to keep on moving forward…" Meg trailed off.

"The answer lies in your meditation practice, Meg. Every time you sit down to meditate you are letting go of everything, and accepting what is in the here and now. Quite simply the more you meditate the more stable and in control of things you will feel."

"Sometimes, though, if I'm completely honest, I get so worried about the future. I can wake up in the middle of the night and spend hours worrying."

"Well, that's really not good. I'm going to show you a technique that I use to remind me to come back into the present moment and away from those debilitating thoughts. How do you place your hands when you're meditating?"

Meg placed her thumbs and forefingers together and placed them on her knees.

"OK, you use the classic yoga mudra, that's great, and you place your hands like this every time you meditate?"

Meg was nodding her head in agreement.

"Brilliant. When you gently push the tips of your thumb and forefinger together you are stimulating the pituitary and endocrine glands, which enhances concentration and dissolves stress. It can even prevent insomnia! In addition to that you associate this hand position with the periods in your life of the most clarity and peace which, when used in times of stress, will remind your brain of feeling calm and you can reprogram your mind to feel more relaxed."

"Wow, Jo, that's so simple, even I can remember to do that!"

"It's easy, Meg, I teach it to children and we call it our magic button, and they use the technique in the classroom with great success. It will help to bring you out of negativity and back to now, a reminder to be aware. Then you can bring your attention to your breath and let go of your stress with your exhalation."

Meg feels grateful for the technique as she walks back to

her room and promises not just Jo, but *herself* that she will use the magic button and meditate daily.

Thinking outside the box

Finally in comes Joss who has never heard of a vision board before.

"Hi Joss, come in and sit down."

"Thanks, I have to say Jo, I am intrigued by all this vision board business."

"And is there a specific area that you'd like to look at?"

"Well, I'm just feeling really happy to be on home soil right now and spending some quality time with loved ones. It feels fantastic to just be here, although it is a massive culture shock. At the moment I can't see further than that!"

"That's really lovely, Joss, to be in a place where you appreciate your friends and family so much. But what does being here mean to you, long term?"

"Well I need a job and I wont be able to live with friends forever."

"Where would you like to ultimately live?"

"I've always wanted to live on the south coast and be close to the sea."

"That's a great start for your vision board Joss. You can find images of suitable properties online and just print one that you love and stick it on your board, it's that simple."

"Cool, I can do that."

"What about work?"

"Well I have a container arriving from Thailand in a few weeks which has stock from my shop that I wanted to sell here."

"How are you going to do that?"

"I don't know, maybe online."

"Anywhere else?"

"Ehm…it would be good on a market stall, Camden or somewhere."

"Great, sounds perfect."

"In fact, I have a friend who knows someone that manages Spitalfields Market!"

"Could you call them?"

"Yes! I don't know why I didn't think of that before!"

"Brilliant, Joss, you might even have your market stall before the stock arrives!"

They laugh and Joss is amazed at how easy it is to get into the swing of getting yourself organised and designing your dream life.

Half way through

Saturday evening's class is focusing on working the shoulders and hips, followed by a very loud gong wash.

"The hips hold the past, folks, so this could be quite an intense session for some of you!" Jo was there for support, so no one felt too alarmed by this information.

After their beginning meditation and seven full rounds of alternate nostril breathing, Jo gets the group opening their hips from all different angles.

"OK, sit with your legs out wide and spine straight. If you can't get your pelvis upright then sit on a block." Some of them do this. "Then activate your feet in Tadasana (Mountain pose) so that your legs and back feel strong. You should feel the stretch down the inside of your legs."

"Not half!" Rob squeaks.

"Yes, it's a very deep stretch, but one that if practised regularly will open quickly, so this can be your yoga homework, to do this when watching the TV!"

The group laughs and promises Jo that they will do their homework. The session ends in a shoulder stand, with some of them resting their legs on a chair in Halasana (Plough pose), some in full Sarvangasana (Shoulder stand), and Grant and Meg doing some variations too.

New healthy recipes

"Tonight's a treat, we're having healthy fish and chips!" Dominic exclaims as they all congregate hungrily in the kitchen.

The conversation around the dinner table is positive und upbeat, with everyone getting along brilliantly as healthier eating options are discussed. The all-time great dinner of English fish and chips has been served that evening in a way none of the others have seen before. Dominic has steamed salmon with herbs, and sweet potatoes have been baked, not fried. It is delicious, and served with steamed peas, carrots and spinach.

A movie follows about the power of the mind and quantum physics. The gang settle into the huge luxurious sofas and Dominic makes some fresh mint tea.

Afterwards Jo sleepily asks:

"We have the option of moving our schedule one hour back in the morning to give everyone a Sunday lay-in, or we can keep the timings the same as today. Hands up for an extra hour in bed?"

Everyone's hands shoot up in an instant and the whole room erupts with laughter.

"Good, that's settled easily then! See you all in the morning at 9am for our first session. Sleep well."

Really getting in to it now

"Morning everyone," Jo breezes through the door and sits on her cushion next to her singing bowls and gong.

"You should all feel that the sun salutations are much easier today than the previous days, as the body is now getting into the rhythm of the timetable. Unfortunately it's our last day together so I really hope you can incorporate this morning practice into your daily routine at home. You will get massive benefit."

Jo leads them through the Vinyasa (flow) and the following quiet meditation where the mind rests on sound.

"I can't believe how much easier that was today," Sam tells the group.

"Yes, I agree totally," Rob replies.

"I feel totally different now to how I felt just 24 hours ago," says a pleasantly shocked Joss. "I need to do more yoga!"

Closing session

Dominic's fruit smoothie is delicious again and everyone fights for seconds. There is disbelief from Joss, Grant and Sam as they go upstairs to pack their bags, no one wants to leave later in the day. There is just one more session and one more meal before departure.

The final session is stabilising and balancing. Jo begins.

"You have a handout in your folder with pictures of these postures that we are doing today. They form a good basic practice for you to take home with you. You have your sun salutations in the morning, and then you can do these standing postures after. Mixed with some balances you are good to go!"

They perform Trikonasana (Triangle) and Virabhadrasana

(Warrior) 1, 2 & 3 along with Vrksasana (Tree) and Ardra Chandrasana (Half moon).

"OK, let's now sit down in Baddhakonasana (Cobblers pose). How do everyone's hips feels after last nights session?"

"I think it's going to be tomorrow that I'm going to ache," Sam shares.

"Yes, I think that is quite possible," Jo agrees.

The session finishes with half handstands against the wall, then a very quiet breath meditation and Jo sounds the singing bowl for the last time.

"So that's it! The weekend is over once we have had our lunch. I really hope you have all enjoyed your yoga and meditation, and that the weekend has been a success."

"It's been magical, Jo, thank you so much," gushes Joss. "I will have to come to the next one, or see you in between if it's possible."

"The retreats are run regularly, and I have top up day-long workshops too at my studio."

"That sounds great, I'll definitely be in touch."

There are a few tears as the gang start to roll their mats up. They walk to the huge kitchen where Dominic has made a fabulous lunch and some of the group share contact details.

"I have to say you've been a great group and it's lovely to see that some of you are going to stay in touch." Jo comments.

"I think I can say for the group that we are all grateful for your attention to detail and support throughout the weekend Jo," Grant states.

"Here, here," agrees Joss. "Dominic the food has been amazing, and Jo the teaching inspiring. I feel great."

"Thank you, everyone. You guys can do one last thing for me, though. Fill out the questionnaire again, rating how stressed you feel now and name some emotions you have at this time."

"Yes, no problem Jo, top marks now I think!" says Rob.

Not the end, this is just the beginning!

"The weekend has flown by," says Meg.

"I know, I could really do with another couple of days. My body and mind has only just got into the swing of the timetable and now it's over!" replies Joss as she struggles with her oversized holdall.

"I wish I could feel like I do now, all the time," ponders Rob. "How long will it last, Jo?"

"Well, that's up to you Rob. If you can continue to do a little meditation everyday, just 5 or 10 minutes, then that will top up how you are feeling now and you will feel better able to deal with stressful situations. And the more effort you put in, the better the results so some sun salutations, standing and balancing postures, breathing exercises and meditation will all keep you feeling like this. Welcome to my world!"

"You're so lucky, Jo!" replies Meg, "I wish I could have your life!"

"So if that is what you want Meg, make it happen. No one is stopping you from having the life you dream about, other than you!"

"I know, I know!" Meg laughs.

Chapter Seven

Jo

Epilogue

"Our deepest fear is not that we are inadequate. Our deepest fear is that we are powerful beyond measure. It is our light, not our darkness, that most frightens us. We ask ourselves, 'Who am I to be brilliant, gorgeous, talented, fabulous?' Actually, who are you not to be? You are a child of God. Your playing small does not serve the world. There is nothing enlightened about shrinking so that other people won't feel insecure around you. We were born to make manifest the glory of God that is within us. It is not just in some of us; it is in everyone. And as we let our own light shine, we unconsciously give permission to other people to do the same. As we are liberated from our own fear, our presence automatically liberates others."

Nelson Mandela

Although the character names in this book have been made up, their stories are very real and come from my direct experiences.

I truly believe that I would probably be dead now if I had not stumbled across yoga and meditation all those years ago. The practice has changed my life for the better and taught me that anything is possible. It has given me the confidence to leave a desperately unhappy and unhealthy relationship, and battle my many addictions.

Today I am married to a wonderful man, who does the cooking at some of my retreats – we make a great team!

In fact, I can honestly say I feel I have it all, and because it has not always been that way, feel like I have a winning formula to find happiness, success and love. I want to share this formula with as many people as possible. My retreats, *and this book,* are based on it.

Winning formula

Yoga and meditation have picked me up and lifted me out of a world of despair.

My practice has nurtured and supported me through all the rough times and I have emerged, like a lotus out of the mud, up into the sky.

Now I want to show others the path that I have taken, which has transformed my life into one full of love, happiness and abundance.

Unlocking your future

I believe that everyone has the potential to find and live in happiness. We all have the capacity within us for a contented life.

Most of us, however, have covered this natural state up with our addictions, stress, anger, resentment, busy lifestyles and a belief that we are not worthy of happiness.

So, we must find a way of peeling away the layers of conditioning and the expectations that we place on ourselves, and those of others. Get in touch with how you really feel so that you can discover the gem of how life can be, if only you let it!

Years back I felt like I was in a locked cage. I could see that life was beautiful on the outside, but was not able to reach it. Slowly, bit by bit, I have dug my way out of this prison. It has been dirty, difficult and painful work, but so unbelievably worth it.

My favourite analogy of the potential we all possess is of a diamond. A diamond in its natural state does not look particularly beautiful at all. It can be found in mud, and looks like a simple rock. But when it is worked on i.e., cleaned and polished, it is the most beautiful, special object *and we all have beauty within us.*

Getting unstuck

It is my experience that we get 'stuck' very often. I have been stuck in various jobs, relationships and addictions. It is how to extract yourself from these destructive patterns that I now have experience in.

Take love relationships, someone in an abusive relationship will repeat the behaviour with one partner after another, if they do not realise the pattern. As the abused, being a victim is often the only role they have ever played, having never experienced a life without treading on eggshells. "But I love him," is often the response when a woman takes back a man who has cheated on her, not realising she has just given him the green light to repeat his behaviour.

We must all set out our own boundaries. How do you really want to be treated by your partner? What actions are acceptable and unacceptable. Then communicate these boundaries to your partner, *and stick to them!*

The abuser on the other hand if allowed, will find no

reason to not play out abuse in every relationship. Perhaps they have witnessed this kind of co-dependant relationship growing up and view their behaviour as 'normal'. The abuser will need someone they respect highly to point out that their conduct is in fact unacceptable, for them to be able to move through this pattern.

The addictive cycle is similar. I myself have bounced from one addiction to another, each one holding me in a tight grip of darkness, until I finally have the strength to push through to the other side. And once through, it is difficult to understand why it hadn't been done before, but the dark oppressive tunnel of being in the thick of an addiction is very hard to penetrate.

So what IS your dream?

Sometimes people are so stuck in a situation or mindset that they just can't imagine a better life for themselves.

I do understand that for some people when I say: "What is your dream?" it takes a while for them to fully comprehend what that could mean to them. I have students who can't think of anything that they'd like to change because they don't think they deserve any better.

But slowly we can change our attitudes and beliefs and the cascade of unlimited possibilities can start to infiltrate our lives. Small baby steps that when continually taken, lead us further towards our dreams.

I feel empowered to know that I am creating my own destiny, and can change the script and employ new actors (and sack the old ones!) whenever I choose. But you have to know what your dreams are for them to manifest and the vision board is a great tool to get you thinking. Have your vision board somewhere visible so that you can see it every day and remind yourself where you want to be. Get yourself into the mindset of being there already, or knowing that your goal is close by. Maybe it's lurking around the corner, just out of sight and remember the more you believe, the closer you get to your dreams.

Starting to see the evidence

When I changed the way I viewed the world and myself in it 20 years ago, I did so not really knowing where or how I could do this. The trust and belief was there that I could take back control of my life, but it was pretty scary in this new world as I was completely out of my comfort zone. However, slowly the trust has built up over the years as I see the evidence stack up and I become happier and healthier.

It's a bit like a seesaw, though. Sometimes we have to take a few steps backwards before we again can catapult ourselves into our new positive, happy lives. And those steps backward are an important part of the process as we then have a reference point.

Start with small goals, ones that you can really imagine blooming. This will build up your confidence. Once you have some evidence, then you can create a bigger goal. The key to the success of this method is your absolute belief that you can realise your potential, and that *you deserve it*.

My conscious evolution

Gradually over the years I am trusting more and more that everything is OK just as it is. I am trying to release my tight grip of control over things that I cannot control.

I now understand that I have control over how I live my life – my conscious evolution – but I also know I cannot control other people and life's situations.

We must all experience sadness, loss, ill-health and unhappiness as well as love, abundance and happiness to live in this world, it makes us human. The important thing is how we deal with life's challenges. We can feel like a victim and moan, "Why does this always happen to me?" or, accept what life throws at us and learn from it.

Taking responsibility for me

I was a victim for years in unhappy relationships/jobs/addictions, and I can say from experience that it's an unhappy and stunted way of living. Then when I began my new life and started changing my reaction to my experiences the victim in me disappeared and I became strong, motivated and inspired. Now I am happy and empowered. I have enough confidence to let go of people and situations that do not nurture and support me. I don't worry about the loss of a negative friendship, because I will be happier without it. Instead I choose to have fewer friendships, but all of them positive and uplifting, and I have more time to spend with these special people.

Limited to unlimited

I continue to swim upstream against the current of society's expectations of me. I have stopped smoking, drinking, drug taking and partying so that I feel peace inside. This has not been easy as the desire to be what I value goes against what my friends are sometimes doing and what society believes to be true as a whole.

Very often I have felt that I was denying myself, so I must keep checking in on my own morals and beliefs, even when they do not match up to those around me.

I have struggled back and forth between what I have always been and what I wish for myself, knowing that when I am kind and listen to what my mind and body want I feel amazing, and when I give in and follow the crowd, I end up feeling disappointed, unbalanced and unhappy.

Drinking alcohol is a perfect example here. Our whole society is woven with the belief that alcohol makes a situation better. Celebrations, commiserations, relaxation, a confidence boost, these are all situations we are led to believe, that alcohol plays a part in.

The ugly truth is that alcohol is a poison, and ruins lives. But take a look in any greetings card shop and take note of how many cards have a bottle of bubbly on the front to show us how much 'fun' drinking is.

I can confirm to the reader that for me, it is much more fun remembering every detail of the party, every conversation that I had there, and how much I can enjoy the next day without a hangover!

I now refuse to accept that I *must* drink champagne to celebrate marriage or birth. I now refuse to accept that I *must* drink myself stupid when something awful happens, because I know that I will feel 10 times worse in the morning!

Over the years I have realised I must listen and honour myself and not just do what everyone else does, to the point that now I have the confidence and love for myself to do what is right for me. I now have strength, I now am who I want to be, and have no regrets as everything that I've experienced to date makes me who I am and becomes the building blocks of my future.

Awake at last

What's happened to me over the past 20 years is that I have

woken up. I no longer blindly believe what society and my peers tell me, instead I work things out for myself.

Through my meditation practice I find stability and can connect to my true self. My true self tells me when I am feeling OK and when I am off balance. The key obviously is to stay balanced as much as possible!

Alcohol just had to go for me as it toppled me over on many levels, and the ensuing abstention has allowed me to feel fully awake.

Start now!

It doesn't matter what you are going through at the moment. You can decide to have a better, more positive life starting from today. Tap into your inner strength and pull yourself from unhappiness and create the life you have always dreamt of. We all have this diamond potential inside us, *all of us*. We just need to find a way of locating it, nurturing it, polishing it up, then wearing it with pride!

Find your creative outlet

I have made this journey with the loving help of yoga and meditation which might or might not work for you. You may find balance through gardening or walking or drawing. It doesn't matter what your passion is, just find it!

When you have something you love doing in your life it gives you something to get out of bed for and can motivate you beyond belief. Surround yourself with inspiring people and relieve yourself of the others. Go on retreats, to workshops, holidays and enjoy your life!

Life is about to become easy, fun and exciting.

This way of living makes me feel free, and I am so grateful

for every second of every day. I feel so lucky that I have found this happiness, freedom and peace which comes from *within me*, and is available to share with everyone in my life. I don't find happiness through other people, happiness emanates *from me*.

My motivation to write this book comes from this place. I see how my students are changing their lives and living their dreams, and I want everyone to know my method to do this. I've done it, my students have done it, and now you can do it too!

About the Author

Jo De Rosa really does have it all. A
wonderful husband, successful business,
loving and supportive people around
her, and she is happy with herself and
her reality.

But it wasn't always like this, and Jo
has pulled herself from an unhappy,
desperate world to contentment,
abundance and happiness.

Jo knows that it is possible for us all to achieve this. It is her
intention through this book, by sharing her own experience,
that you too can find some strength and belief that you really
do deserve to realise your dreams and live a happy life.

She leads retreats, workshops and classes passing on the
knowledge she has gained, and has started work on her next
book. Jo now lives in England with her husband Dominic, his
three children, and their two cats.

Inner Guidance

yoga ● meditation ● detox

Jo teaches yoga and/or meditation retreats, workshops and classes around the world. She also gives inspirational and motivational talks.

Jo can be booked to speak or teach at your event through the following email address:

Jo@InnerGuidance.co.uk
www.InnerGuidance.co.uk

If you want to get on the path to be a published author by
Influence Publishing please go to
www.InspireABook.com

Inspiring books that influence change

More information on our other titles and how to submit
your own proposal can be found at
www.InfluencePublishing.com

CPSIA information can be obtained at www.ICGtesting.com
Printed in the USA
LVOW08s2259180913

353058LV00003B/18/P